PAINTING FURNITURE

JOCASTA INNES

A HOW-TO GUIDE TO AN ANCIENT CRAFT

PHOTOGRAPHY BY ANDREW TWORT

PANTHEON BOOKS, NEW YORK

TO OTTILIE

ACKNOWLEDGEMENTS

SENIOR EDITOR: ISOBEL HOLLAND

CREATIVE DIRECTION: PHOTOGRAFT

DESIGN AND ART DIRECTION: ROB THORNEYCROFT

STYLIST: MARIAN PRICE

SET AND FURNITURE PAINTING: MATTHEW USMAR LAUDER

PRODUCTION CONTROLLER: CHERYL COOPER

The publishers wish to thank the following organizations for their kind permission to reproduce their photographs:

Camera Press: 15, 16; Christie's Colour Library: 10, 13; National Motor Museum: 19; National Trust Photographic Library: 9; Victoria & Albert Museum: 21

AUTHOR'S ACKNOWLEDGEMENTS

The author would like to thank the following maestros for their generous assistance, ideas, information and help: Patricia Richards, Robert Campling, Marianna Kennedy, Jim Howett, Belinda Ballantyne, Lesley Ruda, Matthew Usmar Lauder, Nemone Burgess. Thanks also to the Charleston Trust, Charleston Farmhouse, Firle. Nr Lewes, Sussex.

FIRST AMERICAN EDITION

Library of Congress Cataloging-in-Publication Data
Innes, Jocasta
    [Paintwise]
    Painting furniture: a how-to guide to an ancient craft/Jocasta Innes.
    p.   om.
    Original title: Paintwise.
ISBN 0-679-40620-4
    1. Furniture painting.   I. Title.
TT199.4.I56   1991
749—dc20   91-52653
                                              CIP

Produced by Mandarin Offset
Printed and bound in Hong Kong

CONTENTS

FOREWORD 6

THE PAINTED BACKGROUND 8

THE PRACTICAL ASPECTS 22

SIMPLE TRANSFORMATIONS 38

COMMODE A LA MODE 40

OAK OFFICE FURNITURE REVIVED 46

A COMB AND BRUSH UP FOR A VICTORIAN CHEST 52

HOW TO CRACK 'CRACKLE' 58

GLOSS OVER A JUNK TABLE 64

MARBLING MAPPED OUT 70

A PINE BOX GOES UPMARKET 76

DOODLING FOR REAL WITH PENWORK 82

THE AGEING TREND 88

CUSTOMIZED WITH COLOUR 94

TROMPE L'OEIL TOPS A TABLE 100

A SPARKLING SPONGEDOWN 106

WICKERWORK AWASH WITH COLOUR 112

A RASH OF COLOUR 118

MASTERCLASS 124

WRITING ON THE TABLE 126

IN THE FOOTSTEPS OF DUNCAN AND VANESSA 130

THE GOTHIC SCREEN 134

SCANDINAVIAN STYLE 138

CAVE ART COMES TO TOWN 142

PATRICIA RICHARDS' ELDORADO 146

HOMMAGE A HENRI 150

THE WITTY BRUSH 154

INDEX 158

SUPPLIER'S INDEX 160

FOREWORD

By all accounts the do-it-yourself phenomenon is on the increase. And this despite, or perhaps because of, a downturn in many national and domestic budgets. The urge to try one's hand at painting adventurously, as I know from the response to my books and products (Paintability Stencils, House Style Decorating kits) is surfacing in countries, like Italy and France, where paint effects are still a novelty outside what one might call the 'international set.'

People love decorating their homes, and tackle jobs like painting walls and woodwork themselves, to save money. But they paint furniture, it appears, for slightly different motives, to try out ideas in a small way, to add a splash of colour, or just for fun. It is perfectly understandable that beginners feel more relaxed about trying their skills on relatively small items. A transformation job on a blanket box or a kitchen cupboard is a weekend sized project. It won't interfere with family activities, doesn't cost an arm and a leg, and if it doesn't turn out the way you hoped, a rescue operation is no big deal. On the other hand if it is a wild success the knock-on effect is out of all proportion to the scale of the venture. Marble a job lot of kitchen chairs and preparing food becomes more pleasurable, stipple a verdigris finish on wire baskets, ordinary flower pots (even plastic ones) and your thumbs turn greener, and I don't mean with paint! These are just a couple of our limbering-up exercises for beginners, from the Simple Transformations section, but don't imagine that because they are easy to do the results look elementary. No one is going to believe that your penwork mirror, or your *faux* marquetry chest, was the cinch you tell them it was. Simple effects can be very sophisticated. But it is good to keep setting your sights a little higher, and this is where the Masterclass section comes in, with its account of more advanced techniques handled by professionals, working for the most part on commission. No one pretends that reading what the experts do makes you an expert, but it can teach you a lot; what the problems are, how they cope with them, the preparation they take for granted, and the short cuts they stumble upon.

Jocasta Innes

LONDON 1991

THE PAINTED BACKGROUND

Every culture worthy of note has produced its own style of painted or decorated furniture, and we need an historical context to evaluate what we see and like. This introductory section briefly examines some of the most significant and influential developments in the long history of this friendliest and most domestic of the decorative arts.

FRIENDLY DECEPTION; THE *FAUX* FINISH FAMILY

The discovery that paint could be used to counterfeit rare or costly materials must be almost as ancient as art itself. In one sense art is about faking, creating three-dimensional space and light, on a two-dimensional canvas. Marble and wood grain were already being imitated by painters in Roman times.

Renaissance love of splendour gave new importance to the skills of the decorative painter. The walls of churches, palaces and villas were decorated with *trompe l'oeil* architecture framed in painted marble. Italian painters or *depentori* have always been exceptionally skilled at marbling, favouring the theatrical effects often more spectacular than the real thing. A good painter would be able to produce fast and impressive painted versions of at least half a dozen main types and colours of marble – grey carraras, yellow sienas, breccias in red and purple brown; combinations of these can be found dramatizing the simply plastered walls and columns of country churches all over Italy.

The chief intention behind all *faux* finishes is to make surfaces look more impressive, to pass off a cheaper substance – plaster, softwood – as a more expensive one and to create a more visually exciting design or texture. Almost every precious or visually exciting natural material – tortoiseshell, malachite, lapis, porphyry – has been mimicked in paint, a highly effective way of enhancing and enriching furnishings as well as walls. Being practised in a range of these *faux* finishes clearly gives the decorative painter almost unlimited scope for creating new effects.

Some of the most popular for furniture and knick-knacks are tortoiseshell and malachite, vivid and handsome materials which can be imitated with remarkable success with transparent glazes and varnishes. The dazzling green and black variegations of malachite are counterfeited by drawing on a piece of torn cardboard through wet glaze. Painted tortoiseshell can be the glowing tawny and brown of the natural shell, or the sophisticated mottled reds and greens which the cabinet-maker Boulle devised by backing translucent polished shell with solid painted colour. He used these to veneer the surfaces of desks, cabinets, tables and clocks, producing an effect of great richness. Inevitably this was soon imitated in paint. To some tastes the painted imitation, the poor man's Boulle, is more attractive than the version it is copying.

Arte povera is the term used to describe 'poor man's art' in Italy. One of the most appealing examples is the fake lacquerwork of the 18th century, using hand-painted cut-outs – predecessors of the Victorian 'scraps' – glued down over a painted base to suggest the lavishly coloured surfaces of early Oriental lacquer. By building up so many layers of varnish that the stuck paper seems level with the surface quite a convincing lacquer effect is obtained.

Penwork, in which surfaces are elaborated with pen and ink decoration, is another example of a captivating fraud. Penwork was a hobby of artistic amateurs in the 18th and 19th centuries, an impressive, versatile way to add interest to all sorts of surfaces. Penwork makes a decorative painted inset. Extended over an entire piece in the style of carved ivory it looks astonishing, heirloom material. Penwork was usually inspired by engravings; bands of scrolled penwork might frame a vignette copied from Claude Lorrain or Nicolas Poussin.

Rustic graining is a technique that was much used to give a slap-up effect on provincial furniture during the 19th century, and it is becoming popular again today as people find how simple it is to do and how jolly and impressive it can look. The 19th-century graining bonanza was a direct consequence of the immense popularity of Cuban mahogany, with its exotic black figuring and warm, glossy chestnut colouring. Fashionable among the wealthier classes in the late 18th century, it was being imitated with paints and glazes on modest softwood pieces by the 1820s, and mahogany graining is still one of the finishes most often found on cheap 19th-century chests of drawers and other cottage pieces, especially in Scandinavia and the USA. The bold abstract patterns made by some of the earlier examples are not like any known wood, but are undeniably striking and handsome. Rustic graining effects are achieved rapidly, another reason for their continuing appeal. Painters used a wide variety of glazes based on beer, vinegar, or any fluid that had a bit of 'stick', and created their patterns with all sorts of found materials from corks to corn cobs. The glazes, usually tinted brown or black, were brushed quite thickly over a base coat in red or ochre, depending on the tone required, and then distressed while wet. Some grainers achieved highly convincing imitations, using combs, floggers and other tools of the trade, but as a striking finish for a rustic piece it would be hard to improve on the rustic grainer's figure of eight combing or corncob sunbursts.

The revival of painted finishes for furniture has led to a renewed interest in the whole family of *faux* finishes, from *trompe l'oeil* witticisms enlivening standard kitchen pieces (such as lengths of painted string curling out of drawers) to lavish *pietra dura* effects on table tops. A newer type of *faux* finish spectacularly renders the scars of age and wear, the grazing and peeling away of colour which so often appears on old painted pieces. Heavy distressing is currently the favourite effect with young designers as well as with firms specializing in

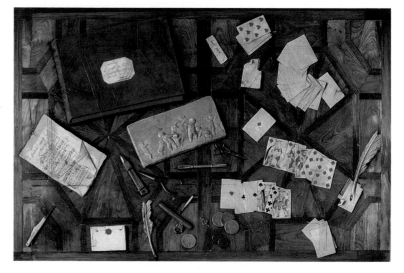

Above: Trompe l'oeil *of this startling verisimilitude – not one of the objects on the marquetry table is real – takes the art of the* faux *finish as far as it can go. Compositions like this one seem to descend from the* pietra dura *exercises where lifelike scenes were created with a mosaic of marble and semi-precious stone.*

high-class reproductions. There are various ways of achieving the right look, most of them involving the use of water-based emulsions or acrylics, a point in their favour since it enormously speeds drying times. Sometimes two emulsion colours are superimposed, the top one being rubbed with wire wool or sanded down (or wiped hard while wet) to let the colour beneath show through. This gives richness of colouring. Brushing emulsion colour over dark stained wood and rubbing back on mouldings and leading edges and round handles to reveal the dark wood convincingly counterfeits the wear and tear on an old painted piece and can give a cheap whitewood repro piece something of the battered charm of old country furniture in an impressively short space of time. Crackleglaze, a substance which creates a bold *craquelure* or alligatoring, is becoming popular because it too gives plain surfaces a complex texture suggestive of age and wear.

THE EASTERN INFLUENCE;
TRUE LACQUER AND JAPAN

A certain amount of confusion surrounds the early history of lacquered furniture in Europe, but one thing stands out clearly; the first appearance of this brilliantly decorated, flawless Oriental material created something of a sensation in 17th-century fashionable circles, and the consequent demand for it had a far-reaching effect on the development of painted furniture as a whole. Some of the confusion derives from the name 'coromandel' applied to this type of lacquer. This is misleading, since the work was of Chinese manufacture, whereas Coromandel was the name of a town in southern India whose only possible connection is that the East India Company used it as a trading post. However, from the perspective of Europe, the Orient was so mysterious that one name was as good as another as long as it had a fine, exotic ring to it.

Coromandel is a type of lacquered product which first appeared in China during the Qing Dynasty (1644-1912). In contrast to the carved red lacquer of the Ming Dynasty, something of an acquired taste outside China, Qing lacquer is immediately appealing with its colourful painted scenes unfolding across a lacquered background of sumptuous smoothness. As with all true Oriental lacquer the surface was built up with as many as 100 coats of 'lac', the sap of the tree *Rhus vernicifera* found growing in parts of China. One of its peculiarities is that freshly applied lac must be dried slowly, in dark, damp conditions; it is somewhat toxic, causing skin complaints among the craftsmen who work it. Conscientious application, burnishing and abrading between layers with a paste made of powdered deerhorn, creates a remarkable surface with a deep lustre reminiscent of a mineral like jet rather than anything man-made. To these attractions was added the picturesque elegance of typical coromandel surface decoration, showing images which were to be copied interminably under the heading of 'chinoiserie' – curly-eaved pagodas, humpback bridges, plum blossom, cranes, robed mandarins in pointed

Above: Dating from the early 19th century, this pair of sabre-legged side chairs in darkest black and gold, is an especially captivating example of japanning, the European craftsmen's imitation of Oriental lacquer. The little vignettes shown on the chair backs, in gold leaf and coloured paint, could well have been copied from Stalker & Parker's celebrated treatise.

hats. It is easy to understand why this exotic import took the fashionable world by storm and, despite every effort by the Chinese traders to step up production (inevitably leading to a decline in workmanship), demand far exceeded supply.

Meanwhile European craftsmen had not been idle. It was hardly to be expected that they would be able to reproduce a manufacturing process involving exotic substances on the far side of the known world, but by trial and error a method was arrived at of building up a paint surface which superficially resembled true lacquer, being smooth and glossy, with a depth of colour previously unknown in painted decoration. The chief element in this new process was a thin, clear, rapid-drying varnish made from insect excretions encountered on another Oriental tree. The name of the tree may have misled the painters into supposing that they had stumbled on the source of true lacquer. At all events the substance used was called shellac and, no doubt with a view to cashing in on the vogue for exotica, the new process was called after another remote and legendary spot on the globe – Japan.

Japanning, and by extension japanned furniture, filled the gap in the market satisfactorily and japanned wares were soon so popular, and curiosity about the process so intense, that John Stalker and George Parker thought it timely to produce a book explaining how to 'japan' as well as supplying several pages of suitably Oriental patterns for japanners, amateur as well as professional, to copy. Their book, *A Treatise of Japaning and Varnishing*, published in 1688, soon ran into several editions.

One of the interesting results of the orientalizing craze was that japanning became a fashionable pursuit among artistically inclined upper-class people who would not have dreamt of painting furniture in the ordinary way of things. Young ladies amused themselves painting boxes, writing tables and other pretty items according to the instructions given in the Treatise, often, no doubt, with gratifyingly attractive results. A well-prepared surface was given many layers of coloured varnish then decorated with lively scenes copied from the Treatise, often using egg tempera. Finally, when the paint was quite dry and hard (a slow business with egg tempera), the object was given a great many coats of shellac, smoothed and refined with agents such as rottenstone or powdered pumice, to create a peculiarly glowing depth of colour and a sparkling gloss.

While falling short of true lacquer's perfection, japanned pieces have a gaiety and brilliance of their own, enhanced if anything by the naivety of much of the 'sharawaggi' ornament. (This word was coined by the English architect Sir William Chambers, who had visited China as a young man, to describe chinoiserie ornament.) Japanning also lent itself to a wider colour range than did lacquer and European cabinet-makers and painters exploited this advantage, producing furniture in admirable colours, from pale ivory as in Chippendale's painted and japanned suite for the actor David Garrick to a sumptuous peacock blue, taking in crocus yellow, light red, pink, grass green and chestnut brown en route, and, of course, the original black and deep red, whose popularity was undiminished. Gold and silver leaf, in various tones, was often combined with japanning; it was usually laid over the slightly raised areas of a design which japanners achieved – in imitation of coromandel – with layers of gesso. Further decoration would be added in oil colour or egg tempera before the final application of shellac.

All the great 18th-century cabinet-makers produced some japanned pieces, notably Thomas Chippendale in England, Duncan Phyfe in America, and the Martin brothers in Paris. 'Vernis Martin', made to a laborious and secret formula, represents technical perfection as regards japanning; the little double-sided desk created by the Martin brothers for Madame de Pompadour, in the tenderest of blues decorated with raised gilt ornament, must be one of the most enchanting items of furniture ever made.

Enthusiasm for japanning continued unabated throughout most of the 18th century, but with the rise of Neo-Classicism and a more 'correct' taste in the latter part of the century output began to decline, enjoying a last Indian summer in such fantastical buildings as the Brighton Pavilion.

Interestingly enough, the 20th century's flirtation with immaculately smooth coloured surfaces in furniture took a step backwards, away from mass production. Eileen Gray, one of the more innovative designers of the century, began her career as apprentice to a Japanese craftsman in order to learn the art of working with true lacquer in the traditional way. Her magnificent lacquer screens, cabinets and other items are lacquer at its purest, devoid of ornament other than its own flawless texture and deep shine.

POLITE PAINTED FURNITURE;
THE ARISTOCRATIC TRADITION

Though the evidence is necessarily scrappy, given the relative fragility of painted surfaces, enough remains to establish that painted furniture has been a prized status symbol for thousands of years. All the ancient civilizations – China, Egypt, Rome, India, Persia – seem to have given painted pieces a special place. Colour had an importance to the ancient world transcending its value to us today. Painted colour combined with gilding, stencilled ornament, carving and inlay, gave a rich and splendid result, and was often used for ceremonial pieces, thrones, couches and tomb furniture.

During the Middle Ages the Church was the greatest patron of the decorative arts, and the gorgeousness of ecclesiastical furnishings influenced the tastes of the laity; brilliant heraldic colours remained popular, often allied to shallow relief carving and much gold leaf. During the Renaissance, painted furniture appears to have lost ground; richly carved oak and walnut, polished rather than painted, seems to have been favoured instead.

For a while the European craze for elaborate marquetry inlay ousted all other forms of decoration on furniture. But then the first pieces of eastern lacquerware began to arrive, and its immense popularity leading to European imitations like japanning and 'Vernis Martin', (see page 11), undoubtedly helped restore painted furniture to an important role in elegant interiors of the day. Indeed, refined and elegant, as opposed to rustic, painted furniture, was produced in greater variety, with more finesse in the 18th century than in any other period before or since. By this time furniture itself had changed, becoming lighter, more delicate in shape and line, with a fine-boned air quite different from the massive ponderousness of earlier centuries.

As social life became less formal, interiors too moved away from the stiff grandeur of earlier aristocratic houses, towards a more intimate, convivial atmosphere. Furniture that could be easily moved about, for cards, conversation or the newly fashionable tea-drinking, became increasingly popular; much of it was made of painted pine, with caned seats.

Colours changed during the 18th century, the strong hues of the 17th century giving way to a softer, flowery palette including buff, French grey, pale olive, stone or that peculiarly 18th-century shade known as 'drab'. Uniform colour was relieved by decorative additions, painted by the skilled craftsmen employed by leading cabinet-makers. These might be a simple lining and a painted vignette or elaborate, with posies, garlands, knots of ribbon and graceful husks or bellflowers descending slender tapered legs. The lighthearted prettiness of painted furniture suited the somewhat fantastical decorative styles – rococo, Gothic, chinoiserie – that prevailed throughout the century.

Eighteenth-century designers like Robert Adam developed the idea of interiors planned down to the last detail; colours, hangings, plasterwork and furnishings were integrated visually. Painted furniture lent itself to this co-ordinated look as it could be decorated en suite with the room, as shown by the elaborately decorated chairs and firescreen designed by Adam to complement the lively Etruscan Room at Osterley Park.

Painted furniture has a family resemblance wherever it comes from but some national traits emerge even so. The Italian palette is warm and exuberant, with glowing yellows, greens acting as a foil to brilliant garlands and lavish gold leaf. French taste was more subtle. Translucent washes of colour over gesso gave greyed pastels – faded pink, powdery blue and green, mustard yellow – a subdued glow, over which decoration aimed at a fragile prettiness. The English tended to favour sober colours – buffs, drab, grey, olive – enlivened by lining, grisaille and touches of gold. The Scandinavians painted furniture to disguise the fact that it was made from indigenous pine and fir.

Above: After the brilliance of japanning, the general trend in polite painted furniture in the 18th century was towards a refinement and subtlety perfectly exemplified by this very elegant and feminine Louis XVI side table. It has a marble top and paintwork ostensibly cream but which is actually a complex and indefinable colour that has been glazed, shaded and lightly touched with gold.

Late 18th-century Gustavian furniture has a distinctively cool, restrained look, matt pale grey, with relief carving – a knot of flowers, ears of corn – picked out in chalky pastels. American taste followed the European lead, with a preference for bolder contrasts and stronger colours.

Most high quality painted furniture was produced in capital cities, and gradually copied by provincial craftsmen, often using the 'drawing books' or 'pattern books' compiled by people such as Sheraton, Hepplewhite, Jean Pillement or the self-styled Professor of Ornament, Matthew Darly. Technically, 18th-century work reached a consistent standard of excellence; skilled labour was cheap enough to produce work

to a standard that would be uncommercial today. Many thin layers of paint (all hand ground) were applied over a foundation of gesso and abraded to give surfaces fine and hard as jasper ware.

The Empire or Regency gave a new direction to furniture painting. Pieces became plainer, dark colours – black, dark green, maroon – set off gilt and '*faux* finishes' such as graining, bronzing and porphyry.

The Victorian age is dominated by buttoned upholstery and mahogany. From this time onwards painted furniture tends to be 'designer' furniture, designed by architects such as William Burges, Philip Webb and Edwin Lutyens or designers such as William Morris, and painted, in some cases, by artists of the calibre of Burne-Jones. Inevitably it was expensive and was created for a small elite. The social and cultural conditions which had allowed so much painted furniture of quality to be produced during the 18th century at competitive prices had departed irretrievably. So long as furniture painting adhered to the painstaking old ways with slow-drying traditional media applied by hand rather than by mechanical spraying equipment, it was bound to remain out of step, and broadly unprofitable, in the age of mass production.

Over the past decade or so, painted furniture has undergone a modest renaissance. Reasons for this include: an extension of the general trend toward decorative surfaces, a reaction against the banality of stripped pine, a search for the personal touch in decoration, growing use of man-made materials such as MDF (medium density fibreboard) which require painting and a new openmindedness about ways to achieve a pleasing result cost-effectively. The young avant-garde adopt technical innovations with enthusiasm; the trend is toward illusionism, fun rather than heirloom material which in a fashion-led age makes considerable sense.

BY THE PEOPLE FOR THE PEOPLE; THE FOLK OR PROVINCIAL TRADITION

Little painted furniture of the humbler sort – the marriage chests, carved stools, bride spoons and spoon racks which commemorated peasant alliances throughout Europe for centuries – dates back further than the 17th century.

Poor people owned little furniture; what they had was basic (tree trunk stools) or built-in. The earliest item commonly found among European peasant societies is the marriage chest. These survive all over Europe, vividly decorated, and bearing the names of the bridal pair and the date of their wedding. One has to look to the 18th century to find a characteristically popular style evolving, with the bold colouring and stylized decoration which sets such painted pieces apart from furniture produced for the upper classes.

Peasant furniture attracts all sorts of misconceptions about itself. Its decoration gives an effect of exuberant spontaneity, as if some colour-starved farmer or farmer's wife had suddenly been run away with by the brush. Painted decoration at this level was almost always executed by professional or part-time craftsmen, sometimes itinerant but more often working out of a regional workshop. The decoration was essentially imitative, based on colours, effects and motifs peculiar to village, town or region, which were reproduced by generation after generation with little modification.

Another surprise is that almost all the motifs and effects were originally imitated from aristocratic models of a generation or so earlier. The time lag is typical. Peasant art was slow to assimilate new ideas but hung on to them long after they had lost favour in the fashionable world. Baroque and rococo elements were still being used in the folk repertoire well into the 19th century.

Every country has its own tradition of vernacular furniture, but what we see in our mind's eye when we think of folk decoration was largely produced during the 18th and 19th centuries in the northerly, conifer-growing countries stretching from Russia across central and eastern Europe, Scandinavia, and finally the northernmost swathe of the USA and Canada. The forests provided the inhabitants with cheap softwood for building and joinery. This led naturally to paint, as protection and to give a more expensive effect, and also to provide peasant homes with cheering bright colour. It also influenced the style and shape of the furniture itself, typically simple, generous and sturdy. Storage was a problem in crowded peasant homes, so chests and, later, armoires were important items. As peasant societies grew more prosperous they extended their cottages, adding extra rooms, an upper storey, making space for more furniture. Tall-case clocks, bureau bookcases, chests of drawers, wall-mounted cupboards, immense bedsteads and sofa beds were all pieces prized for their dignified, upper-class associations. The 'conifer culture' produced national variations, yet what is more striking is a powerful family resemblance; shared characteristics include bold colour, preference for symmetry and surfaces crowded with pattern. The most popular motif in all countries, at all periods, is the stylized flower piece, used on chests, door panels, bedheads, chair backs and seats and clock cases.

Another universally popular decorative feature is scrolling brushwork based upon rococo fronds or the more regular, and classical, anthemion.

Though similarities seem to outweigh differences, there were local differences sufficiently marked for an expert to be able to look at a decorated piece and determine where it was painted. Sometimes the colour scheme provides the clue, sometimes the use of a particular ornament, sometimes a style of marbling or graining in a particular colour combination.

Brilliance rarely degenerates into garishness, partly because of the limitations on a palette relying mainly on natural earth pigments, partly too because a peasant painter possessed an instinctive skill in the handling and massing of colour and ornament. Little peasant decorative work appears weak and irresolute. Indeed, gutsiness is the word that best sums up the vitality of vernacular painted pieces.

Colours changed as chemistry produced cheap new pigments like Prussian Blue, magenta and other aniline colours. But the most popular colours always remained warm brown red, ochre yellow, a sludgy green and thundery blues. Adding that useful tint of age and dust, raw umber, to colours is one easy way of arriving at the right mellowness of hue. Or this can be supplied by finishing with a glaze (usually linseed oil plus turpentine) tinted with one of the darker colours used on the piece.

Milk or casein paints fixed with limewater were durable and their constituents were conveniently to hand in farming country. The itinerant painters who roamed the countryside with a backpack of essential tools and materials made use of what was cheap and local – buttermilk to bind, animal blood or crushed berry juice to tint, soot and lampblack to make grey and black, egg yolk for tempera decoration. Stencils were cut from leather, paper or linen. All craftsmen working in country districts learned to grind, mix and colour paints, bind squirrel or hogs' hair to make brushes, and collect cuttle bones for rubbing down paint; this formed the expertise of their trade before mass production and DIY products arrived. The most satisfactory furniture paint, durable and rich-looking, was mixed from linseed oil, turpentine and pigment, and this was used by professional craftsmen on important pieces. The snag to oil-based paint is its slow drying time. Because of this a task that might take six hours to complete had to be spread over days or weeks – feasible in a workshop but awkward for the itinerant painter boarding with his clients.

Much of the awkwardness, or naivety, of vernacular painted

Above: What people love about antique 'folk' painted furniture today is an elusive quality that might be defined as soul; scuffed, battered, riddled with worm, their exuberant decoration crazed, blackened or hanging in shreds, they nevertheless give off a powerful atmospheric charge of an earlier age.

decoration can be explained by the rarity of visual references at this social level. The only book families commonly owned was a Bible, and the crude but lively woodcuts used in many 18th-century editions must have provided images for countless country painters to borrow, and embroider upon.

Many of these anonymous craftsmen were expert and skilful within their limitations. The deft brushwork of a Norwegian rosmaling painter can teach anyone a great deal about brush control, just as the handsome colour combinations of a Tyrolean cupboard or a Pennsylvania Dutch dresser are full of information for people intent on decorating a kitchen. But what makes folk painted furniture so perennially appealing is a heartfelt quality, a gaiety and exuberance, which seems to bring it bouncing off the walls.

FLOWER POWER

It takes no great effort of imagination to understand why flowers have been the most popular theme for decorative painting for thousands of years. Their variety, beauty, and above all their colourfulness, made them an obvious choice. Real flowers fade, but painted they bloom for ever.

People painted the flowers they knew best. The rose and daisy are to medieval Europe what the lotus was to Ancient Egypt and the paeony to China. The Greeks in classical times seem to have leaned more toward leaves and berries – ivy, vines, myrtles and acanthus. Roman flower painting survives in wall-painting at Pompeii, where swags of flowers and greenery link airy painted architecture. But the most ardent flower painters of ancient times were the Persians, whose miniatures and manuscripts of the 14th and 15th centuries abound in painted flowers, used as borders, starring the boughs of fruit trees. One recognizes mallow, rose bushes, almond blossom, dark purple-blue periwinkles. Mogul painters took inspiration from this vision of an earthly paradise 'enamelled' with brilliant flowers, and a last echo of it is found in the vivid floral mosaic still used by painters in Kashmir to clothe boxes and other artefacts.

The degree of botanical accuracy has always varied according to the artist, the period, and the convention. Decorative painting followed the lead given by fine artists. In late medieval times, before perspective, chiaroscuro or realistic modelling revolutionized art, flowers were represented frontally, springing from the ground in neat tufts, larger than life, as in the Cluny tapestries, where maidens and unicorns dally on meadows studded with wild flowers.

The Renaissance ushered in a new sophistication in all the arts, and the technical advances of Post-Renaissance artists gradually percolated down into the decorative work executed by the modest, largely anonymous, tribe of skilled craftsmen or tradesmen – *depentori* in Italy – who were responsible for

Above: Would-be-symmetrical flowersprays add colour and decorative impact to this 18th-century Scandinavian cupboard painted in a pretty, fragile pale blue and creamy white. Note the concentration of wear at much-handled spots – this is the sort of effect painters re-create today to suggest age.

carrying out painted finishes and embellishments on the painted furniture which had become newly fashionable in the wake of a craze for Oriental lacquer.

Paler, prettier colours – ivory, jonquil yellow, pale green, deep blue, used as background colour over a whole piece, made a perfect foil to further painted decoration. On the lighter, elegant furniture, the pretty writing tables, cabinets, '*bonheurs du jour*' (a small desk) that began infiltrating fashionable boudoirs in the 18th century, floral subjects were an obvious choice; garlands and swags were combined with fluttering bows, artless posies or more formal bouquets, while wreaths, pendants and flower and leaf borders became part of the decorative painters' standard repertoire.

These were painted with a naturalism and refinement of

technique very different from the earlier, formalized flower decoration of the Renaissance. The sumptuously detailed flower pieces painted by Dutch masters such as Bosschaert had set new standards of flower painting, both in botanical accuracy and in the loving depiction of the grace, beauty and variety of individual flowers and species.

Translated into decorative painting, the Dutch approach becomes more impressionistic. Botanical accuracy is subordinate to the need to compose a graceful and pretty subject to complement a particular piece. It is a convention of decorative painting, especially furniture painting, that painted detail is added discreetly, flattering the proportions of a piece without setting up rival claims for attention. Flowers used decoratively look more appropriate rendered in light, almost sketchy brushwork.

There was a vogue for flower painting directly on to pale, polished wood, usually satinwood, whose silky blonde texture set off painted decoration well. Chairs associated with the English cabinet-makers Hepplewhite and Sheraton often carried painted floral decoration on their backs. These were sometimes partnered by demi-lune tables with painted garlands running round the top edge. The flower painting on such items is often executed with extra care and skill, perhaps by a senior painter attached to the firm. This was a period when drawing and painting were regularly taught to fashionable young ladies and amateurs often became highly accomplished. It is not unlikely that the same ladies who amused themselves japanning small pieces according to Stalker and Parker (see page 11) completed their work with carefully rendered flower studies.

Decoupage of printed flowers, hand coloured, and stuck to the painted surface before varnishing many times over, gave a similarly appealing touch which made fewer demands on artistic talent. Mrs Delaney, the gifted widow of an Irish clergyman who became a dear friend to Fanny Burney and the daughters of George III, became famous in her day for her cut paper flower pictures of exquisite delicacy, and the bulk of her collection is now in the possession of the British Museum.

The Victorian era preferred mahogany and plush to painted chairs with caned seats, but flower decoration survived, indeed flourished, on the black and gold papier mâché work called Pontypool Ware. The typically sparkling black and gold scheme admirably set off vivid handpainted flower pieces, roses predominating, which were often given an even richer glow by being painted with transparent glazes over petal-shaped insets of mother-of-pearl. The style of these floral decorations seems to owe something to the compositions featured on the Berlin work patterns which were another ladylike craze of the time, featuring rich clusters of roses and other flowers in brilliant colours.

Painted flowers play a subordinate role in the decorative schemes for furniture designed by William Morris and Co and frequently painted by Burne-Jones. These are stylized flowers, in the medieval manner which the Pre-Raphaelites so admired; clumps of daisies, periwinkles and violets were depicted rather in the manner of medieval herbals.

Floral decoration has never entirely gone out of fashion, but perhaps the last important name to become associated with a decorative use of flowers was the Glaswegian designer Charles Rennie Mackintosh, whose stencilled rose, a one-dimensional and highly stylized abstract of the flower, has become one of the quintessential images of the Arts and Crafts Movement. The Mackintosh rose, thought to have been inspired by one of his wife's appliqué designs, was a single delicate motif which he used to centre a wall panel, or one of his elongated chair backs, or a cupboard door. It was painted in pale shades, non naturalistic, as a rule on a background of white.

UNTOUCHED BY HAND;
THE PERFECT FACTORY FINISH

Flawless surfaces have always been admired and sought after, a form of perfection both visible and, especially, tactile. Burnished metal, woven silk, shaven lawns, polished wood, high-fired porcelains – all these evoke the awe with which most people greet an apparently simple thing taken to its uttermost limit of perfection.

Oriental lacquers (see page 10) were obviously the first instance of this breathtaking perfection in the realm of applied finishes other than gold leaf or enamelwork. Ever since imported lacquerware first arrived in Europe in the 17th century, painters, craftsmen and inventors have experimented with different techniques and materials which might approximate the gleaming purity of texture of the original. This is a branch of endeavour separate from the attempt to re-create its picturesque pictorial charm and colour; here we are only concerned with the basic distinguishing mark of true eastern lacquer – its sumptuous gloss, unrivalled by synthetic materials. Lacquer must surely have been the inspiration behind a whole tradition of skilled trades and crafts whose chief aim was to create a shiny adamantine surface with paint that would look as if it had come into being without human intervention.

Japanning (see page 10) was a first step along the road, a training in the use of layered varnishes and ever-finer abrasives (from coarse glasspapers to the finest powdered pumice or rottenstone) to give a glassy smoothness, though lacking the depth of shine characteristic of lacquer. Nor is a japanned surface nearly as durable; shellac, its main constitutent, is brittle and sensitive to atmosphere, and easily marked and stained. However, the principle behind japanning – many layers of tinted varnish rubbed and smoothed to silkiness – led in its day to the respected trade, or craft, of coachpainting, whose apogee was probably reached some time in the mid-19th century with the development of opaque oil-based paints with a high gloss – enamel paints – used in conjunction with

tougher, oilier varnishes which could take a finer burnish and give a more resilient and durable finish. These, executed in the dark Brunswick greens, purple browns and shiny blacks of the period, relieved by the finest of freehand painted coachlines (made by liners of varying length wielded by unerring hands) in gold or red or cream, probably represent the perfection of paint viewed purely as a slick and flawless covering, handsome in its own right. The contribution made by this technical advance to the mechanical inventions of the age – steam locomotives, hansom carriages, sewing machines, not to mention the wonderfully appetizing and shiny world of mechanical toys – has never perhaps been properly appreciated. Their direct heirs in the modern world are the hand-finished car bodies of the 20th century, their innumerable layers of brushed, sprayed and abraded paints and varnishes, smoothed with 'cutting' agents and polishes, worked up to an immaculate, enviable and inimitable gleam.

Pontypool wares of the mid-19th century, of papier mâché or tin, coated with asphaltum, black paint and varnish and baked for strength and resilience, were another example of the pursuit of a perfect surface, though these were as much prized for their superficial glitter of gold powders, mother-of-pearl inlay and gaudy painted motifs.

Stove enamelling, where sprayed-on paints were subjected to heat, thus making them ideal for stoves, kitchen units and bath tubs subjected to ferocious wear and tear, was a later development which is still with us, unrivalled for durability but almost impossible to restore once the glossy skin has been punctured and rust has crept in. As the 20th century advanced, with its Bauhaus-inspired leaning towards mass production as the intelligent modern solution to quality at low cost, a factory finish, based on sprayed paints, varnishes or lacquers, began to seem the ultimate in practical but attractive coloured surfaces for all manner of objects from Art Deco cocktail cabinets to

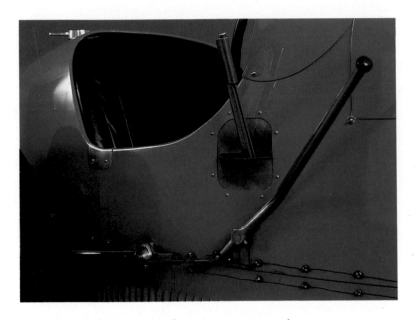

Left: The deep sparkle and lustre of the cornflower blue bodywork on this 1924 Bugatti sports model show the flawlessness aspired to by 20th-century sprayed-on finishes and lacquers. It is doubtful, however, that purely mechanical means can ever quite rival the quality of finishes where some hand work, rubbing down and burnishing, has combined with spray paint and varnishes. Car cutting compound, used by some professional furniture painters to burnish final coats of paint and varnish, was introduced for polishing up and renovating car bodywork of this standard, because the compound effectively polishes off the outermost paint surface. It follows that the car in question must have received numerous coats of paint.

costume jewellery. Items for treatment pass along a conveyor belt into separate sealed compartments, where fine and even layers of paint or lacquer are sprayed over them for a genuine 'no hands' finish. The prevalence and comparative cheapness of such factory finishes seems to have devalued them latterly, but it is clearly only a question of time and innovative talent before some new variant on the theme brings them roaring back into fashion, because they are practical, durable, good value and a disguise for man-made substances.

Ironically enough, the latest development in the area of flawless finishes, based on spray paints and acrylic resins, is a highly successful contemporary version of the oldest perfect finish of all – true Oriental lacquer. Using the latest paints and varnishes together with traditional decoration and motifs, specialist painters have discovered ways of imitating the surface of old lacquer in a fraction of the time it took to apply 40 to 100 finely abraded coats, and thus at a fraction of the price that such a process would cost today. If it lacks the mysterious 'living' quality of true lacquer, it has almost the same toughness and flawless gloss.

EXCEPTIONS TO THE RULE; THE NAMES IN PAINTED FURNITURE

Furniture painting has traditionally been regarded as a trade, or at best a craft, rather than a serious branch of the arts, and its practitioners have tended to remain anonymous, shadowy figures in the history of furniture and interior decoration. But there have been exceptions; court painters, artists and designers have turned their talents to decorating furniture from time to time with results that stand out on grounds of originality and technique. It is unlikely that a painter of the stature of François Boucher took his purely decorative painting efforts, the fans and bibelots for court ladies, very seriously. On the other hand any professional responds to a challenge, a new situation. Court painters were always required to produce a certain amount of occasional work on demand, rather as a Poet Laureate has to compose celebratory odes on royal occasions, and this might range from designs for embroidery to suites of tapestry hangings, or panels of japanning to completely enclose a little boudoir or cabinet. *Trompe l'oeil* commissions, being skilful as well as striking, were probably the most popular with the better known painters, because they could be executed without loss of face.

More often though it is the name of the designer who plans a decorative scheme which is remembered rather than that of the painter who actually carries it out. Robert Adam is more famous than the Cipriani brothers or Angelica Kauffmann, and William Burges is certainly the first name that comes to mind in connection with the wonderful, elaborate pieces of painted furniture he designed, rather than that of his commissioned decorative painter.

Painted furniture was only one element of Adam's integrated decorative schemes, but his taste and inventiveness helped to raise it to a new elegance and sophistication. The simpler painted pieces of the 18th century are perhaps the most attractive to modern taste, and Adam was as skilled at working

in this vein as in the much more elaborate and showy style of, for instance, the Trophy Room at Syon.

The name of Frederick Crace, whose firm was responsible for so much of the decoration of the Brighton Pavilion, is only just beginning to be properly recognized. Crace's former obscurity is in sharp contrast to the fame of John Nash, the chief architect, but by no means the only designer involved. Crace must have been especially concerned with the production of painted decoration, his firm's speciality, and it is becoming clear that he deserves more credit for the quality of the decoration there than had been previously supposed.

William Morris, William Burges and Charles Rennie Mackintosh made their contributions to painted furniture at the drawing board rather than with the brush, but all of them set their individual mark on the evolution of painted furniture (among much else) during the course of the 19th century.

Mackintosh was much influenced by the refinement of Japanese art and design, but the brash young designers who made up the influential Omega Group drew their ideas from primitive art, fauve painting and other artistic trends of the time. Roger Fry, Duncan Grant and Vanessa Bell were all fine artists who saw nothing wrong in painting furniture – indeed made a special point of doing so as part of the inventive and amusing interiors created by the Omega Group during the 1920s. They created a new and very personal style, using chalky, vivid pastel colours, a gay and flippant line, and a deliberately irreverent treatment of classical notions, for example caryatids, and ornament. Their work is often decried as amateurish, and technically at least it falls way below the exacting standards of professional decorative painters or coach painters; the 'Bloomsberries' had neither time nor inclination to fill and smooth and sand and varnish a piece to flawless perfection. On the other hand their impatience was creative, their colour harmonies were fresh and daring, and the insouciance and charm of their decorative work strikes a welcome note among the austerities of modernism.

The name of Eileen Gray is associated with lacquered rather than painted furniture and the strength and purity of her lacquered screens, or the bateau bed lined with silver leaf which she designed for a Parisian hostess, could hardly be further removed in style from the Omega painters. What Eileen Gray brought to painted furniture was perhaps a new appreciation of the beauty and elegance of a simple perfect finish, unadorned. Many other designers of the 1930s, notably Rateau, who designed an exquisite suite of rooms for the couturiere Jeanne Lanvin, and Ruhlmann, cultivated the sleekness of lacquer in the more expensive Art Deco furniture, inlaid with ivory and ebony, or exotic palisander wood whose dark figuring recalls the zebra- and tiger-skin upholstery which was all the rage at the time. Curiously, despite the sense of apparent frugality conveyed by the idea of modern design, this particular expression of it is based upon the most luxurious and costly materials.

Two other designer/decorators of the 1930s, Syrie Maugham and Betty Joel, used paint for furniture. Syrie's famous all white look (actually dozens of shades of off-white) made much use of ivory enamel paint. Betty Joel favoured colour, the daring mauves and oranges that still seem so Deco today. Interior decoration was a chic occupation for society women, and Syrie Maugham's chief rival was Sybil Colefax, who set up a small but exclusive decorating firm with John Fowler. Colefax and Fowler has changed over the years, expanding and prospering, in the process losing something of its initial verve, the innovative streak which led Fowler to mix humble materials such as matting and ticking with grand and costly ones. But the painting studio run by the firm continues to produce a significant quantity of decoratively painted items to this day, to perfectionist standards that inevitably make them too expensive for a mass market.

Above: This splendid coffer decorated in polychrome and gold leaf is in the William Burges medievalizing vein, both as to the choice of colour and simple devices like the powdering of gilded stars on the dull red interior paintwork. A combination of tight repeating ornament with passages of looser figurative painting are typical of 19th-century style medievalism.

At the opposite pole from the conservative, well-bred work produced by Colefax come the pieces from a whole crowd of irreverent and individualistic young decorator/designer/ painters who are beginning to make a name for themselves working to private commissions or showing in places such as Liberty or the Crafts Council. Furniture painting seems to be acquiring new status as a decorative art; indeed, some of the more recent productions, taking their cue perhaps from the designs of Emilio Sotsass, are more like eccentric sculpture than useful things to sit on, eat off, or put things in. However, in a commercial scene dominated by the painted effects of the various kitchen design companies, tending towards the traditional and the safe, the anarchic imagination shown by much of the new painted work seems a healthy sign.

THE PRACTICAL ASPECTS

This section covers the processes involved in turning your ugly duckling into a swan. Having found your transformation piece, does it need stripping, filling, sanding, priming, shellacking, paint mixing, glazing, antiquing? For how-to, read on.

PAINTWISE

WHAT AND WHAT NOT TO PAINT

Don't paint serious antiques – but don't paint trash either. Look for the solid wood and decent workmanship of mass-made furniture of the 1920s, 1930s and 1950s. Decorative inspiration could come from the knotty pine of the 1970s, French wirework or 19th-century shop fittings. Check for structural problems, worm, broken hinges, warped veneer, wobbly legs. Wood adds value, but consider metal, resin, MDF, wicker, cane, even plastic. Think big (kitchen units, wardrobes), but also small (lamps, trunks, boxes). Hunting grounds include junkyards, office furniture suppliers, thrift shops, markets, salerooms and skips.

JOB LOT WITH PAINT POTENTIAL

Nothing shown here cost an arm or a leg. The oldest item is a heavily overpainted Regency period picture frame, the newest a sturdy willow basket; the most useful an oak settle, the most appealing a prettily detailed child-size desk in pine which probably began life, stained or painted, in a Victorian schoolroom. These are items with enough character to challenge the imagination, presentable as they stand, but with a potential that the right paint finish could dramatize. Not represented here, but in evidence elsewhere, is the less brush-tingling but

serviceable 'brown furniture' – as the antique trade styles it –
which can look all the more rewarding and rejuvenated after its
paint treatment because it looked so sleazy and unlovable before.
In this category I would number post-war 'utility' bedroom
suites, fake Jacobean varnished oak of the 1920s, all whitewood

much repro, and most of the cheap pine (actually knotty deal)
that crammed every furniture store and DIY shed through the
1970s and 1980s. The role of clever paintwork with all of these is
to upgrade, adding fine colour, texture, a splash of pattern, and
the personal touch.

STRIPPING OFF

If life is too short to stuff a mushroom, it is also too short to spend the amount of time earlier generations of craftsmen devoted to the preparatory ritual of cleaning off, filling, sealing, undercoating or priming which used to be taken for granted in quality decorating work. If you are setting up as a professional decorative painter, you should learn the steps required for a superfine traditional finish. The discipline involved is helpful, and job specifications may demand it. DIY painters are usually in too much of a hurry to be so particular; excess time spent on preparation leads to a waning of enthusiasm and often means projects are abandoned halfway. There is a momentum to decorative work which makes it difficult to pick up again on a project that has gone cold.

Use your common sense. Give each project the preparation time it merits. Restoring a fine antique demands more care than re-vamping junk you may grow out of in a year or two. But remember that careful work looks better longer, and adds value to just about anything.

REMOVING OLD FINISHES

Cleaning an old piece back to bare wood is necessary for only a few of the finishes – liming and staining and Belinda Ballantyne's watery Scandinavian finish (see page 138). For most projects it is adequate to sand or strip off just enough of the existing finish to give a smooth, non-shiny surface to which paint can adhere.

SANDING

Over large, flat areas, a power-driven orbital sander cuts into most finishes sufficiently to provide a 'tooth' for paint. This is fast but it creates dust; lay down dust sheets, wear a mask and old clothes. Progress from medium to fine grade paper, working with the grain. This will deal with old paint, spray lacquer, varnish and French polish.

On small, oddly shaped or antique pieces, use gentler hand-sanding. Move from medium to fine grade sandpaper, cutting it into small squares for easier handling. Use a circular motion, with the grain, a section at a time. After all sanding wipe surfaces clean with a damp cloth.

SOLVENTS

The rule is to use the mildest that will do the job. Solvents are listed here in ascending order of strength.

METHYLATED SPIRIT Use to remove French polish. Swab on the methylated spirit, leave to soften for a minute, then begin rubbing with the grain, using medium grade wire wool pads, discarding these as they clog. Smelly (not noxious, but try to work out of doors) but not too messy and leaves a smooth, bare surface. Methylated spirit also softens old emulsion finishes. Proceed as above.

PROPRIETARY VARNISH STRIPPER Shiny brown finishes which are not French polished probably shift with this stripper, which is gentler than paint stripper. Protect the work area, wear plastic gloves, and rub off with wire wool; otherwise use as directed by the manufacturers.

PROPRIETARY PAINT STRIPPER Dissolves heavy paint encrustations, a layer at a time. Useful on small pieces, blurred by old paint, or on detail on large pieces otherwise finished with a sander. Use as directed. Wear gloves, scrape off softened paint with a scraper or shave-hook, finish with wire wool and neutralize with water plus a dash of vinegar.

CAUSTIC SODA Some firms offer a caustic bath service to strip doors and large items. Caustic soda is effective, but drastic, as it eats away old glues and roughens wood. Use as a last resort. DIY caustic treatment is only for those with a yard, hose and drain nearby. Add 1 tablespoon of caustic soda to

1 litre of boiling water in a plastic bucket. Stand clear until the bubbling stops and the fumes evaporate. Swab the mixture over surfaces with an old cloth or brush. Allow paint to soften, then begin scraping and rubbing with wire wool, hosing down frequently with clean water. Wipe over with vinegar to neutralize. Wear rubber gloves, coat wrists with vaseline and sluice stray splashes on your skin with a water and vinegar solution. The messiest, cheapest way to clean off all finishes.

The fiercest stripping often fails to shift old aniline stain, deeply sunk into wood. Seal with aluminium primer before painting as the stain can 'bleed' through subsequent paint coats.

SMOOTHING, FILLING, PRIMING

Some contemporary paint effects will not need any or much of this. Cracks and craters add to their rustic appeal. However, pieces to be given a smooth, traditional oil-based finish, need special attention since their surface flaws have a way of looming larger. Anything to be given a *faux* lacquer finish should be super smooth, thoroughly filled and sealed.

SMOOTHING

Surfaces roughened by caustic soda or stripper should be sanded with medium then fine grade papers, working with the grain and dusting off until the surface is silky. For a fine finish, continue to smooth in the same way, after priming and after sealing with shellac, and between some, if not all, paint and varnish coats. The finer the finish you require, the finer the abrasive paper you should use. Use wet-and-dry, dipped in water to lubricate, at the final paint and varnish stage. Wipe over rubbed-down surfaces with a clean rag before going on to the next stage. All abrasive papers should be worked with the grain, gently, firmly and evenly, partly to clear dust, grit, hairs and other unwanted attachments, partly to bond and level out the layers of paint and other media.

FILLING

Not as mandatory as when painted surfaces were like porcelain, the filling processes are still handy for smoothing out flaws (screwholes, splits and cracks) and levelling off coarse porous surfaces, like those found with some man-made boards such as chipboard. Fillers come in various proprietary forms, mostly interchangeable, but some with special virtues.

DIY FILLERS Sold for filling interior woodwork, walls etc., these are plastery substances useful also for filling deep cracks and other blemishes. Use as directed by the manufacturer, fill 'proud', sand level, then seal with shellac before priming and/or painting. A fluid mix can be smoothed on with a knife blade to fill in grain before being sanded and sealed with shellac. Neat and useful, these fillers tend to shrink, creating new cracks.

PLASTIC WOOD This is excellent for patching up chipped veneer you want to paint over. Fill 'proud', sand level and seal with shellac. This will not shrink like plaster filler.

PROPRIETARY GRAIN FILLER For overall surface filling of open-grained timber such as oak. Use as directed by the manufacturer.

ISOPON This is superb for filling the end-grain of man-made boards, as on kitchen units of blockboard. Mix as directed by the manufacturer, fill, smooth, sand level when dry, then seal and paint.

FINE FILLING For finishing antiques, use after the first sealer/primer coat is dry to even out tiny blemishes that show up best at this stage. Fill 'proud', level with fine grade paper, seal, then repaint.

PRIMING

Primers underlay most paint systems, filling, sealing and providing a key for subsequent finishes. They can sometimes be dispensed with but, when in doubt, a coat of suitable primer does no harm and may prolong the life of your finish.

RED OXIDE A cheap metal primer that inhibits rust, this is useful as a base for paint finishes on metal.

ACRYLIC PRIMER Extra fast-drying, powdery and easy to apply, this is the all-purpose modern primer, especially for use with emulsion paints. It may need rubbing smooth before painting.

ALUMINIUM PRIMER A problem-solver, this isolates possibly tricky substances – stains, dyes, etc. – that might bleed into overpainting. Metallic and tough, it dries quite fast.

SAND-AND-SEAL SHELLAC Used by some professionals, because it fills, seals, dries fast, and sands to super-smoothness. For fine work.

CHAIRMANSHIP

SERVICEABLE BUT SIMPLISTIC

This where most of us begin, brushing a couple of coats of pale gloss (here bathroom pink) over a boring chair to cheer it up.

SING A SONG OF COLOUR

Bright crimson paint, folksy decoration in yellow ochre (the poor man's gilt) and many layers of gloss varnish transform our basic chair into 'folk lacquer'.

SAME CHAIR – FOUR OPTIONS

Getting clever with paint enables you to make over a piece in manifold ways with interestingly different results. To point up this truth, we show four nearly identical rush-seated chairs of unpretentious rustic style, given four distinct and varied finishes. Each special finish brings out a different aspect of the chair, grooming it, so to speak, for a different social occasion. You'll see that paint can do more than provide a quick cover-up; depending on how you use it, it can make a piece dramatic, thoroughbred or folksy, thus multiplying your options.

TRADITIONAL AND TASTEFUL

Decorators' 'dirty white', given the whole works from fine filling through to discreet blue lining and final distressed glaze, brings out a cool patrician quality.

THE ELOQUENCE OF DISTRESS

Today's favourite battered look is easily achieved by coats of strongly contrasting colours in matt emulsion rubbed back so the undercoat shows through.

Glossed in pink straight from the can, a chair is just a chair, handy for the bathroom, tacky when it gets shabby. But how much more interesting it is when paint is used creatively, as in the three other versions shown. Which finish you choose has to do with the character of the piece, your lifestyle and your home. A fine traditional finish takes longer, goes with everything, wears well. Vivid shiny colour rescues the nondescript and can cheer a whole room, while the battered look is made to order for kitchens that want to go countrified; a set of these, a scrubbed pine table, and the style is set.

TOOLS OF THE TRADE

The selection of decorative painting tools shown here were all used in executing finishes for this book. You would not need so many for a few projects, and many of the items will already be in your toolbox. Long-handled artists' brushes in bristle, and softer hair, are used for decorative brushwork, lining details; one or two of each are enough for most purposes, unless brushes are specifically stated under the list of materials for each project. A badger stippler is expensive, either a standard 3 inch/7.5 cm decorating brush used end-on or a rounded stippling brush as shown can substitute. Two or three widths of standard brush, plus a separate, fine-bristled varnish brush, are needed for applying paint and varnish. Ideally they should not be used with different media but this can be done *if you clean them scrupulously*. First brush off excess paint on paper. Clean oily media off with white spirit, watery media with water, finishing up in both cases with a good scrub in warm water with a squeeze of detergent. Use a scrubbing brush to scrub down the bristles from the handle to loosen paint. Water-based paints are easier to clean, but be warned; any paint deposits left will harden and, unlike oil-based media, are almost impossible to remove with brush cleaner, stripper etc. A varnish brush used with shellac needs immediate rinsing in methylated spirit, then a detergent wash. Keep varying grades of sandpaper and wire wool from coarse to fine.

A WORKMANLIKE SELECTION

Tools that have seen long service are not pristine, but note that while handles, rulers etc. may be paint-smudged, bristles are clean. Aside from stippling brush, graining comb, artists' brushes, marbling goose feathers and stencils this is standard DIY equipment.

1,2,3 Standard decorators' brushes in ¾-3 inch/1.9-7.5 cm widths; 4 Scissors; 5,6 Goose feathers for putting in veins on marbling; 7 Roll of masking tape; 8 Sandpaper in fine to coarse grade, for rubbing down. Wet-and-dry (not shown) is black and also comes in various grades; 9 Scrap of foam torn from foam roller pad, for

sponging and stencilling; 10 Eraser; 11 Scalpel or craft knife with detachable blades; 12 Hard lead pencil; 13 Rotring drawing pen; 14 Felt tip pen; 15 Rubber three-sided graining comb; 16 Natural sponge small enough to fit the hand; 17 Copydex; 18 Wire brush; 19 Heavy duty Stanley knife with sets of blades; 20 Wire wool

in medium and fine grades. Best bought by the roll; 21 Pre-cut plastic stencils; 22, 23, 24, 25 Artists' brushes in sizes 4, 5, 6 and 7; 26 Five soft artists' watercolour sable brushes in sizes 2, 4, 5, 6 and 7; 27 Plastic ruler; 28 Professional quality 'badger' stippling brush with handle on the back.

TRADITIONAL COLOUR

Picking colours for a project is stimulating, because the right colours will not only transform a piece of furniture but will have a knock-on effect on your room scheme. Finding one's way through the hundreds of colour 'chips' on commercial paint charts, however, can be unnerving – the options seem limitless. With practice one becomes more confident but meanwhile, everyone longs for guidance, formulas – the colour equivalent of a good recipe. Colour wheels take one into the realm of optics, and theory is useful for artists but not much help in planning a colour scheme. For a decorative painter, the most useful benefit of knowing which colours are complementary is that one can tone down an overly bright shade by mixing in a little of its complementary. Examples of successful colour groupings used by artists and craftsmen working in different fields provide a more accessible and helpful reminder of colour contrasts and harmonies which can be seen to work. Ethnic colour harmonies, as shown in traditional rug weaves, textiles and pottery, are strong but mellow. For more sophisticated colour mixes, look at 20th-century artefacts – Deco textiles, the celebrated Bakst designs for the Ballets Russes and decorative work by the Omega group. Then there are the historic colour schemes whose effectiveness can be gauged by studying contemporary prints, paintings and furnishings. Currently, the virile but subtle colour combinations of the Baroque period (late 17th, early 18th centuries) as shown opposite, or their rather more vivid Empire/Regency versions, are providing colour inspiration that feels right for our own times.

A SELECTION OF BAROQUE/GEORGIAN COLOURS

All the colours shown here are picked from a commercial range popular with designers and decorative painters. They approximate closely to the colours most often used, in varying combinations, for room schemes and furnishings in the period under discussion. Wooden wainscot or floor-to-ceiling panelling was the norm in more prosperous houses, and architectural detailing – cornices, architraves, moulding – figured prominently, often marbled or grained in bold contrast. Furnishings were sparse, with colour being provided by lacquer pieces, blue and white china and embroideries.

1 Off white

2 Blue-green

3 Stone colour

4 Drab

5 Silver-grey

6 Lacquer red

7 Pea green

8 Indigo or purple-blue

9 Snuff colour

10 Red-brown

Note: These are not the manufacturer's names. Professionals claim they are rarely satisfied with commercial emulsion colours and invariably modify these either with a little contrast emulsion or tinting agent i.e. universal stainers, gouache tube colours or powder pigments.

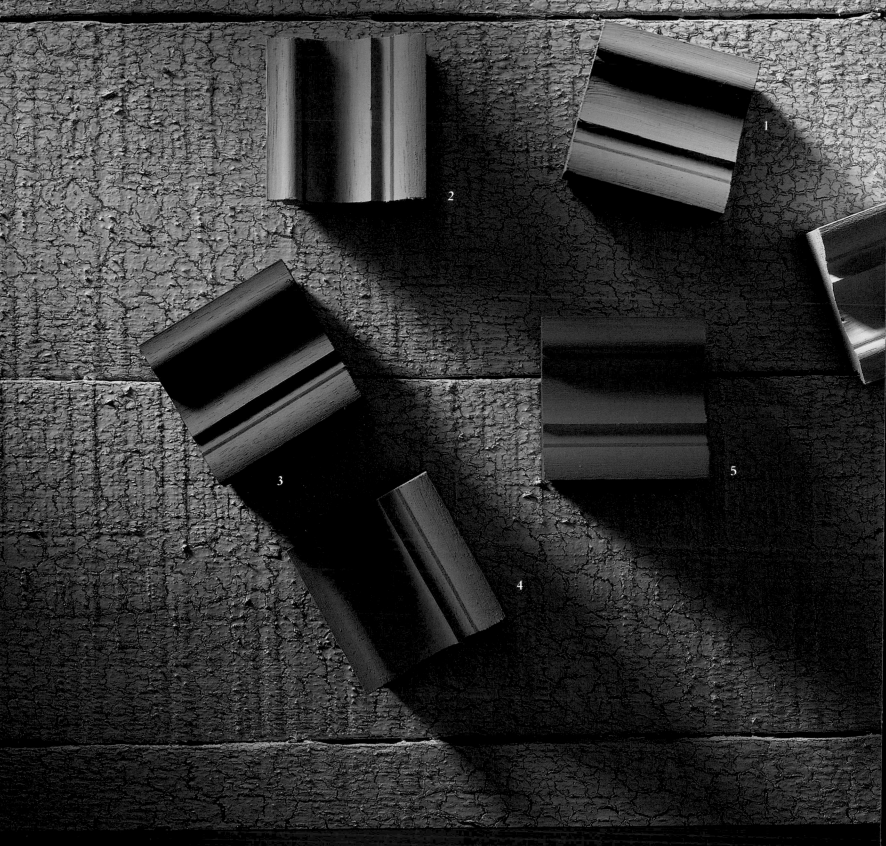

VIBRANT PROVENÇAL COLOURS FROM A CURRENT PAINT CHART

Everyone who has holidayed in Provence, or in any of the Mediterranean tourist spots, takes home memories of vivid, chalky pastel colours ranged along old housefronts, casually daubed on awnings, signs, street furniture, so clean and clear they almost sting the eyes. Fierce Mediterranean sunshine calls up a different palette – resonant hues of green, yellow, blue, tempered by sharp pink, sky blue, arsenical green, faded mauve, piercing cerulean, and for contrast, the sooty black, dark blue or green of ironwork and shutters, the rusty-red of fishing boats, the universal dazzle of pristine white limewash.

OPAQUE COLOUR

Historically, the opacity, or covering power, of paints was usually determined by their chalk content, or the natural opacity of the pigments used. The earth colours – umbers, siennas, ochres, oxides – tend to be opaque, the rarer, unusual pigments – indigo, vermilion, Vandyck brown – more transparent, though the 19th-century discovery of hugely potent aniline colours – Prussian blue, magenta – fudged this rule of thumb. Distemper (often called whitewash), a primitive paint made from whiting or chalk dissolved in water and bound with animal glue, was the first opaque paint in common use. Distemper paints, which could be made up and tinted on the spot from readily available ingredients, were used in many parts of the world for exteriors, interiors and furniture, though their powdery texture renders them far less durable than matt emulsions, their modern equivalent. Decorative painters today are coming to rely more and more on standard emulsion paints, or acrylic tube colours, both of which dry fast and cover well. Plaka casein-based colours are popular with some professionals for their ability to take a 'burnish'. The loss in richness, texture, and liveliness of colour which seems inseparable from these convenience paints is compensated for by various means; inter-mixing colours gives subtler shades and texture can be added by crackle glazes or rubbing down colour over colour. Final richness, a 'fattiness' associated with oil media, can be added with final varnish coats (usually oil-based) containing a little added tinting colour, or by rapid watery colour-washes in deeper shades sealed with varnish, or perhaps with wax, preferably beeswax.

1 Provençal pottery green

2 Ochre yellow

3 Terracotta

5 Poppy red

6 Brick pink

7 Corn colour

Note: These are not the manufacturer's names. (See page 31).

TRANSPARENT COLOUR

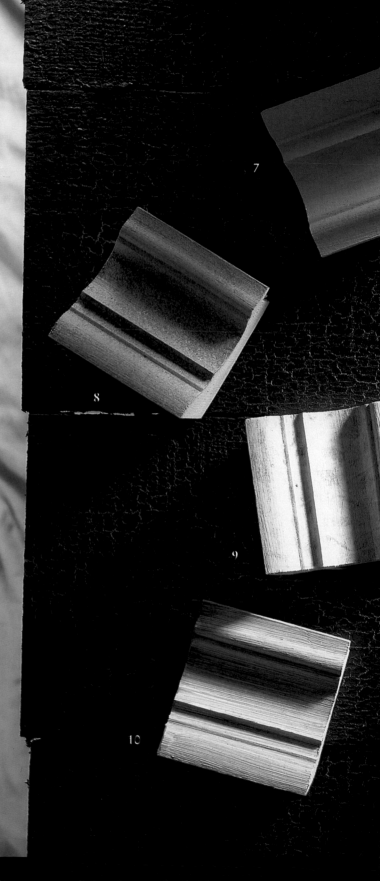

Unalloyed colour, as on the previous spread, is a proven tonic but can be unruly in a northern climate. The colours, in furniture as well as room schemes, which suit cooler climates best are modified, or subdued in various ways, much as the sun appears through a haze of mist; colour tempered in this way is less immediate and rousing, more mysterious and atmospheric. One way to achieve this effect is by 'dirtying' colours with raw umber, the colour of old dust. Another is to build up colours by degrees, using layers of transparent media (glazes, varnishes or washes) over a base which may be plain white, for radiance, or a pale shade of the final colour for depth and mystery. Though identical pigments are used, a completely different effect is arrived at by layering blue-green glazes, or washes, over white than from mixing blue-green with opaque white to give a similar intensity of tone. It is like comparing transparent aquamarine with opaque turquoise. Over today's favourite emulsion paints, thin colour washes (acrylic colours, diluted until watery, wiped on with cloth or sponge) and/or tinted finishing varnish (artists' tube colour oil mixed with polyurethane-based varnish) restore something of the depth of colour and delicacy of texture we have come to associate with the traditional furniture paint system of flat oil paint distressed with tinted oil glaze. Layers of tinted clear varnish (each coloured a little differently) are the modern counterpart of the old craftsman's layers of slow-drying tinted glazes made with linseed oil, turpentine or white spirit and tinting colour.

SOPHISTICATION; NINETIES COLOURS AND TRANSPARENT EFFECTS

Colours to the right of the picture have a slightly acidic brilliance derived from Art Deco textiles but at home in the colour spectrum of the 1990s. We are talking here of colours like lime green, orange, salmon pink, lilac. A little of one or two of these will update a colour scheme, but it needs several working together to really put the message across. The four 'chips' on the left illustrate what can be done with tinted transparent oil glaze applied over the same basic yellow base colour, and distressed in different ways.

Sharply new or subtly glazed
and distressed:

1 Sky blue

2 Scarlet

3 Bronze

4 Salmon pink

5 Lime green

6 Mauve

Glazed colours:

7 Yellow base used for all four chips

8 Base glazed and stippled

9 Base glazed and ragged

10 Base glazed and dragged

Note: These are not the
manufacturer's names. (See page 31).

SIMPLE TRANSFORMATIONS

Modern furniture painting hinges on speeded-up processes which give more impact for less time. Fast-drying acrylic primer, paints and varnish allow a piece to be completed in a fraction of the time needed for oil-based media. Emulsion paint is less durable as a wood-finish (though varnish redresses the balance) but decorating styles change so frequently this may not be a disadvantage. The finishes shown here are quick-change recipes for beginners onwards, using easily available tools and materials.

A	STIPPLING	page 40		H	PENWORK	page 82
B	LIMING & STAINING	page 46		I	VERDIGRIS	page 88
C	COMBING	page 52		J	STENCILLING	page 94
D	CRACKLE GLAZE	page 58		K	*TROMPE L'OEIL*	page 100
E	*FAUX* LACQUER	page 64		L	SPONGING	page 106
F	MARBLING	page 70		M	WOODWASH	page 112
G	MARQUETRY	page 76		N	SPATTERING	page 118

STIPPLING
COMMODE A LA MODE

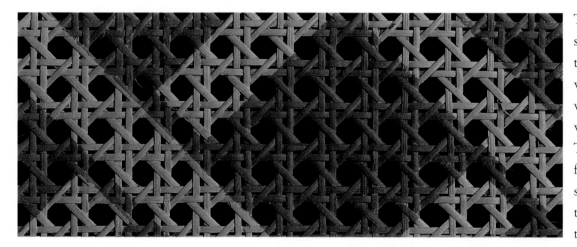

The purpose behind stippling as a technique is to break up the surface of wet paint to give an even, velvety textured colour, without brushmarks. Traditional painted furniture was frequently stippled as a background to applied decoration, and the finish is one that flatters elegant antiques when dramatized by contrast lining, gold leaf, painted floral garlands or stencils. Stippling transparent tinted glazes, one colour on top of another, produces a particularly glowing and mysterious shade of great depth; this technique is often used for walls.

Stippling seemed appropriate as a finish on the striking, throne-like piece illustrated, which is in fact a 19th-century *chaise percée*, or commode, made of teak. Because the bathroom which it graces has quite a bit of mauve in its decoration, the transparent glazes used for the stippling were a pinkish mauve and a greyish brown. Woven cane seats and backs on antique French pieces were often painted, using the background colour of the piece, to give a latticed effect, which is attractive in itself as well as giving a more solid appearance to the caning. This is an easy finish to achieve using strips of masking tape, and was chosen to dramatize the caned seat and back of the commode using the same two glaze colours on to the caning.

The right brush is a considerable help when stippling. A professional stippling brush, specially designed for the job, has a square pad of soft badger hair and a handle on the back, allowing one to exert even pressure over quite a large area. These come in various sizes, from a small brush that

Left: A stippled finish, based on layering oil glazes tinted in harmonious but different colours, makes a smooth professional-looking surface for an antique commode as well as picking up colours in the room decor. A lattice effect creates an attractive trelliswork over painted cane: this was a device often used on French 19th-century painted furniture.

fits nicely on one's hand to a big, heavy brush around 6 inches (15cm) square. Badger hair is used because as well as being fine and soft it has a little 'flag' or split end which picks up paint better and distributes it with greater fineness when stippling.

Most of these brushes are designed for stippling over large areas, hence their size, and because of the badger hair are enormously expensive compared with standard or even artists' brushes. Though a small size would be a nice self-indulgence for anyone who does a lot of furniture painting, there is no real need to splash out on the professional equipment for one or two pieces. Any soft, bushy paint brush or painters' dust brush, used with a steady, jabbing, stippling action, will soften wet glaze or paint and get rid of brushmarks, and a smaller brush is actually helpful on furniture, allowing you to stipple into corners, mouldings and carvings. You may sometimes come across rubber stippling brushes, with flat coarse 'teeth' rather than bristles. These give a very coarse, dramatic looking stipple, sometimes used with textured paint, and are not really suitable for furniture.

MATERIALS

Transparent oil glaze; artists' oil tube colours for tinting; white spirit; paint kettle for glaze; artists' fitch for mixing glaze colour; standard decorators' brush for applying colour; a stippling brush or painters' dust brush for stippling; rags or kitchen paper; masking tape; Craig and Rose Extra Pale Dead Flat Varnish and varnish brush.

METHOD

The existing cream eggshell finish made a good base. (It is best to stipple over an eggshell base because this is non-absorbent and shows up the stipple 'bloom' most effectively. Bare wood would need primer, undercoat and eggshell to prepare it.) A mauve glaze was mixed up first, in the paint kettle, by dissolving a squeeze of tube colour in white spirit and then adding two or three tablespoonfuls of glaze, mixing well.

Test the glaze colour on paper or on the piece to make sure you are satisfied with the consistency and the colour. Harshness of colour can be softened by adding a very little white, either artists' oil tube white or a white oil-based paint, for example undercoat or eggshell. The glaze should be just thick enough to hold the stippled texture – tiny dots of colour – without blurring but not so thick that it looks sticky and dries to a noticeable texture when you run your fingertips over it. Novices tend to make their glaze too thick, thinking of the oil glaze as a sort of paint or varnish instead of a waxy additive which is used in just sufficient quantity to slow the process of drying and give the dissolved pigment enough body to take and hold impressions. Trial and error are the best answer, as ever. It may be encouraging to know that professional painters expect to spend several hours getting a glaze right in both colour and consistency.

First brush the glaze over the surface with a standard decorators' brush, reasonably evenly. Do one facet of the piece at a time and try not to touch wet glaze because it will show fingerprints, though these can usually be stippled over again. Stippling is done with the bristle tips of the stippling brush or the painters' dust brush, 'pounced' or jabbed into the wet glaze over and over until the brushmarks and any unevenness of colour are levelled out and the surface develops the powdery bloom composed of millions of microscopic dots of colour typical of stippling. From time to time you may need to wipe the bristles on a clean rag.

The mauve glaze was stippled over the entire chair except for the caning, taking care to go into mouldings and corners. When

Right: Stippling gives the most even colour and texture, without brushmarks, of any paint finish. It makes a good background to stencilling, or freehand decoration. Stippled glazes in subtly varied tones give a depth of colour reminiscent of japan or old lacquer. Note the use of mahogany graining on the cabinet in the background.

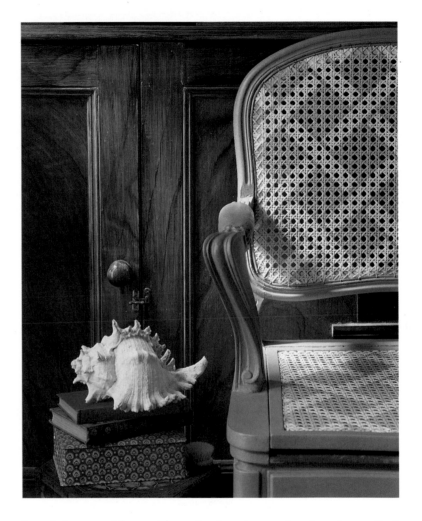

the glaze was dry enough to allow the chair to be handled (usually overnight) a lattice of masking tape strips was applied over the caning as shown and stippled over in the same mauve glaze. This was left to dry. Allow generous drying time at this stage, at least 24 hours, till hard dry.

The next glaze coat was tinted a cool greyish-brown, using white, burnt umber and a little black mixed with the solvent and transparent oil glaze as already described. It was then brushed and stippled over the mauve stipple to soften and cool the colour down and give it a slightly smoky look. It was taken over the caning in just the same way. If the second glaze seems to be dissolving the first, you need to leave the first glaze for longer to dry; once hard dry it will be stable.

The commode was then left to dry for several days before the masking tape strips were removed and the whole piece was given a final protective coat of varnish. It is customary to varnish stippled work with a non-reflective varnish so as not to impair its matt bloom. If any further decoration is to be applied it is sensible to do this over the first varnish coat, so that anything you are not satisfied with can be wiped off with rag moistened in white spirit without affecting the finish beneath the varnish. Lining in particular often needs a trial run, but whatever further decoration you are considering it is confidence-boosting to know that you are not obliged to live with your mistakes. The decorative work will then need varnishing over in its turn.

Left: A two-tone stipple made up of different transparent glazes brings out the crisp detailing on this commode.

STIPPLING IN TWO COLOURS – STEP BY STEP

I. PREPARATION

The commode was already reasonably well painted in a creamy white eggshell. This is the best paint surface for use with any distressed oil glaze effect as it is non-porous. The only preparation needed here was to wash down the old paintwork with a solution of sugarsoap and water to remove grease, and then lightly rub down with fine grade wire wool to smooth off any imperfections in the eggshell finish. Never do more preparation work than you need to provide a good base.

II. STIPPLING COAT ONE

The first glaze coat was mixed with transparent oil glaze, white spirit, artists' oil tube colour in mauve and burnt umber for tinting, mauve predominating. Use a standard decorating brush to brush the tinted glaze over one surface of a piece at a time. Go over this with the bristle tips of the stippling brush, with a 'pouncing' or 'jabbing' action. Do this gently but firmly over the wet glaze till the brushmarks vanish and the colour is an even powdery bloom.

III. A LATTICE OF MASKING TAPE

Strips of masking tape are stuck down, criss-cross, over the canework back and seat, and stippled over in the same mauve glaze. This is left to dry hard before brushing on and stippling the second coat of tinted oil glaze. A brownish glaze was mixed up, using artists' oil tube colour in burnt umber plus a little dot of white, thinned with white spirit till murky but fluid. This was brushed over the previously stippled surfaces, one at a time, and then softened and evened out with the stippling brush. This cooled the mauve finish, and toned in with room colours.

IV. THE FINAL VARNISHING

When the second glaze coat is hard-dry, the strips of masking tape are carefully peeled off the seat and back of the commode, revealing the latticed effect. The whole piece was then given a protective coat of clear matt varnish, which is the most suitable for use over a stippled surface as it retains the powdery texture and 'dry' look. Some painters add a little tinting colour to the varnish itself to enrich the overall colour further. Final varnish hardens slowly over weeks though it is touch dry in hours.

LIMING AND STAINING
OAK OFFICE FURNITURE REVIVED

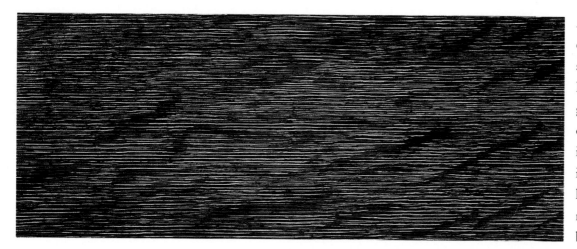

A liming treatment, combined with coloured stain, makes such a handsome finish to open-grained hardwoods like oak, ash and chestnut, that it is surprising to find that its decorative use seems to have come about over many centuries and almost by accident.

Limewash, a primitive paint made from slaked lime, pigment and water, was one of the most commonly used exterior finishes from earliest times, giving glowing colours when mixed with lime-compatible pigments (mostly earth pigments) and an outstandingly dazzling white, which still gives a distinctive radiance to villages in the Greek islands and in many parts of north Africa. Limewash does not wear exceptionally well as an exterior finish (though it is a different story when used over wet lime plaster as for true fresco) but on the other hand it weathers beautifully, softening and fading to those inimitable Mediterranean colours; being fluid, and cheap, it is customarily renewed every year or so, sloshed on with a coarse brush from a bucket, often by elderly black-clad peasant women. Its other peculiarity, unknown to modern opaque paints, is that the colour – white, yellow, orange, blue – becomes more potent and glowing, but not harsh, with every successive layer.

Its use as a decorative finish on oak and other hardwood furniture seems to have been suggested by the discovery that limewashed external beams and woodwork (and Tudor prints show half timbered façades coloured over both plaster infill and timbering) weathered gradually to a pleasing, if fortuitous,

Left: Office type desks are unwieldly pieces at the best of times and this hunky oak specimen looked especially large and looming in its original brown varnish stain, the standard oak finish of the period. But stained deep blue and limed with a white paste that remains in the strikingly decorative oak grain, the result is a desk that looks svelte and contemporary, blending in with a mixture of antique and modern furnishings, as well as the overall blue mood of this ground floor study.

effect, with the residue of white lime powder lodged in the grain giving a silvery, bleached appearance as well as bringing out the natural decorativeness of the grain itself. Oak heartwood, quarter-sawn, produces the intriguing, tigerish configurations, visible on the desk side panels. Filled with white lime powder, these stand out boldly, while the overall timber colour becomes cool, and muted, in contrast to oil based finishes which always bring out a gingery, or bright brown cast.

The idea of combining this white filling with a coloured stain, to arrive at an effect like the one shown on the oak office desk, seems to have originated with the avant-garde group of designers working round the turn of this century in Vienna, and known as the 'Wiener Werkstatte'. Many of them, Josef Hoffmann in particular, began staining oak furniture black, then liming over this, to make subtle use of the natural decorativeness of the wood.

Ambrose Heal designed bedroom suites in natural limed oak during the 1920s and 1930s, and this idea spread through the interior decorating world. Soon people were liming antique oak panelling for new lightness and brightness in stately homes: Oliver Messel, for instance, treated the long gallery ceiling at Parham House, Sussex, to a limed finish. On the whole this is to be avoided today, as the patina of dark oak is irreplaceable.

Recently European furniture designers have been experimenting with other stain colours, as well as substitutes for lime powder. Stain colours are restricted to what combines with the basic (yellowish brown) wood tone – dark blue, dark green, black, maroon. The white grain filling softens the finished colour considerably. For instance the oak desk after staining was a deep blue green (the yellowish tinge of the wood gives blue a greeny cast) but the white filler has lightened this to the colour of faded blue jeans. This gives a helpful optical

illusion on the large, clumsy oak pieces of the early 20th century, with their neo-Jacobean detailing – barley sugar legs, coarse relief ornament. Treated to a gently frosted colourbath, their lumpishness retreats, the old dark looming finish replaced by a matt broken colour which merges easily with the natural textures in a typical 1990s interior. From being glumly downmarket, a piece thus transformed acquires immediate class, its natural grain markings turned to decorative use, its shape and proportions enhanced, and its original dark and treacly surface replaced with one that is subtle and distinguished and easy to live with.

MATERIALS

The desk in our picture was treated using one of the House Style Liming Kits, which include their own stain, as well as a wire brush; liming paste; medium grade wire wool; brush; and instructions. The stain colour chosen was Blue, but it also comes in Black and Maroon. Also needed: medium sandpaper; bleached shellac or white polish; methylated spirit; varnish brush; Craig and Rose Extra Pale Dead Flat Varnish.

METHOD

For liming and staining to take well, two things are needed, a surface cleaned back to bare wood, and the softer grain scoured out with the wire brush. Most old oak of this period was finished with French polish, which responds to swabbing with methylated spirit as a solvent and hard rubbing with medium grade wire wool. Harder cases may need tougher action; commercial strippers, surface sanding with power tools. The closer you get to the natural biscuit colour of raw oak, the better the stain will work.

When the surfaces are clean and clear, they should be sponged over with cold water and left for a few minutes. This softens

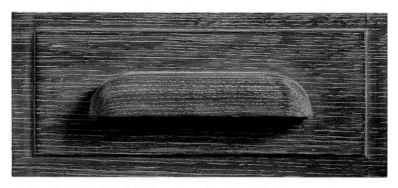

A detail of the finished limed and stained desk.

the inner grain fibres enough to be scooped out by determined rubbing with a wire brush. Wet and brush one facet at a time. Work the brush along the grain, rubbing briskly. In no time a deposit of gunk forms on the bristles, which should be rubbed off on an old cloth or towel. The excavation of grain is minimal, maybe a millimetre or so, but this arduous part of the process should not be skimped because the more grain you clear the more purchase you provide for the white filler, and the more dramatic will be the final effect. Pay special attention, elbow-grease-wise, to areas of heartwood, with boldly striped markings; these become important to the final decorative effect of your piece.

After this fierce wetting and scouring, the overall surface will be somewhat roughened, and should be smoothed by rubbing back with the grain, using medium sandpaper. Brush over the surfaces when dry with a scrubbing brush to clear the grain again. Once dry, apply the stain, using an old clean rag to swab it on generously. Again go with the wood grain. Repeat until the colour looks even and pronounced, a definite colour, not woody. Let dry for a few hours, or overnight. Next apply the liming paste (this is a courtesy title, since the modern filler used consists of inert white pigment, without the mildly caustic

properties of slaked lime powder) from the tub, using the brush provided in the kit, and brushing with and against the grain, to work it well in. When dry the piece will look blindingly white, like an iced cake. But the liming paste is very soft and responds easily to rubbing back with wire wool pads. However, the fall-out is tremendous, and the powder invasive, so try to complete the work out of doors, or on a large plastic sheet, and wrap your hair in a scarf, cover your nose and mouth and wear gloves and old clothes to avoid looking like the Jolly Miller of Dee. Keeping a vacuum cleaner suction hose running helps.

The trick with rubbing off the dry liming paste is to rub hard enough to clear the surface powder, forcing the grain filling powder deeper in, but not so hard that you rub off the fine layer of staining. Start on a less visible surface to get the hang of it; some wood colour re-emerging is okay, but not too much. In cracks, on mouldings, a white deposit tends to be left, quite noticeably; this can be decorative in itself. If you dislike this, use a sharp knife to scrape it off. Rub the piece over lightly with a soft clean cloth to clear surface powder. A slightly damp cloth, or sponge, lightly deployed will clear away still more of the fine clinging film. You will know you have arrived at the right effect when the stained surfaces show up cleanly, with the grain clearly delineated in white as it is on the oak desk.

The finish should be sealed, to seal in the liming and stain and protect it from greasy fingers and handling. One coat of bleached shellac, thinned in the ratio of one part methylated spirit to three shellac, should be brushed rapidly over the limed surfaces to give even coverage. Avoid too much brushing out because it is important not to dislodge the white filler embedded in the grain. After half an hour, for drying, the entire piece should be given one, or two, coats of varnish as this will provide lasting protection.

LIMING AND STAINING – STEP BY STEP

I. BACK TO BARE WOOD

The brown varnish was removed with commercial varnish remover, brushed on, left for a few minutes, then scrubbed off with medium grade wire wool, applied in long strokes with the grain of the wood. It can take two applications of varnish remover to get back to clear, biscuit coloured raw oak as shown here. The paler the wood the better it takes a stain. Next, wet each surface to soften the grain, then scour surfaces with the wire brush provided, working with the grain.

II. APPLYING THE STAIN

Deep blue stain, supplied with the Kit (black and maroon stains are also available) was brushed over the cleaned and scoured oak with a standard decorating brush, repeating till a good depth of colour was arrived at. It may look dark, but remember that the liming treatment will lighten the finish by several shades as you can see by comparing the newly stained drawer with its final version. Liming over unstained wood gives a cool, silvery finish which is popular today for kitchen units.

III. LIMING PASTE DRIES WHITER THAN WHITE

Using the standard brush provided with the Kit, brush white paste, which has an extra thick consistency, over the entire stained surface, working it well into the grain. To do this brush both with and against the wood grain. Though called Liming Paste, in recognition of its traditional forebear, the paste supplied with the Kits is formulated from an inert white pigment, and contains no lime whatsoever. Leave the paste to dry thoroughly. This takes an hour or more depending on weather conditions. A hairdryer will speed this process up.

IV. FINISHING

Use medium grade wire wool pads provided (you will need to provide yourself with more for a large item) to rub off the dried powder on the surface. This is best done outside, on a plastic dust sheet. Keep rubbing smoothly, with the grain, till the stained surface shows through clearly, with the white paste residue deposited in the grain, as the detail on the right clearly illustrates. A limed piece needs to be sealed to make sure that the liming stays in place, and to prevent fingermarks darkening the wood gradually. Use thinned white shellac, followed by standard matt or eggshell varnish.

Right: This close-up of the desk top shows how dramatically the white on dark effect of liming over a stain emphasizes the configurations of oak grain

COMBING

A COMB & BRUSH-UP FOR A VICTORIAN CHEST

This is one of the few techniques in this section that makes use of traditional oil-based media, for the simple reason that glazes based on proprietary 'scumbles' – transparent oil-based glazes – create a layer of colour that remains ductile and obedient to manipulation for considerably longer than water-based media. Their disadvantage is that they are slower drying – from 8 hours to 48 depending on temperatures, how thickly you use them, and so forth. Scumble glazes, usually sold as Transparent Oil Glaze, has a consistency somewhere between honey and old-fashioned hair cream which responds to any distressing technique with a pattern as clear as a thumb print on an ink pad.

The responsiveness of a tinted glaze containing the proprietary transparent oil glaze, as here, is perfect for a strong, almost 3-D pattern like the one produced by combing on our pine box, but beginners should be warned against the temptation to spread the effect over larger surfaces, like walls. Thick, transparent oil glazes over large areas, however distressed, always end up looking like jam – that is, sticky and unsubtle. Professional painters avoid this either by using the smallest amount of proprietary mixture that will still hold an impression (only to be gauged by experiment), or by reducing the quantity of proprietary glaze while at the same time adding a little white paint (undercoat, oil based) to cloud, blur and soften the final effect.

It can be patted with bunched-up rags (as in 'ragging'), plastic bags, crumpled paper, the side of one's hand and, in this case, rubber graining

Left: The rich colours and textures of the transformed pine box make it an ideal partner to other interesting surfaces, an old kilim rug, baskets, a batik picture. Using a gold undercoat gives the ensemble extra glow, and a touch of sophistication. Combing emulsion over emulsion (use contrast colours) looks folksy and primitive.

Left: Feisty as knitting, our combed finish shows up clearly in contrast to the tough metal banding on what looks like a Victorian doll's trunk. The dull lustre of gold paint beneath emphasizes and enriches the texture of this precise, dapper combed effect.

GLAZING AND COMBING – STEP BY STEP

I. PREPARATION

The chest in its original state needed little attention. The wood (a lesser form of pine) had been stripped down already, but the waxing applied to bring out the colour of the wood needed to be cleaned off, use ordinary white spirit and medium grade wire wool, or a proprietary wax solvent. The metal bands round the box were too handsome to paint over. They were simply avoided, any stray paint being wiped off with a rag dampened with white spirit, but to save time you might prefer to stick masking tape over the bands.

II. GILDED BASE

The base coat for our combed finish is a home-made gold paint, made by mixing gold powder (obtainable in a range of colours) into fast-drying orange shellac. The idea behind this was that the subdued glow of the gold paint (never as gleaming as gold leaf) would provide a dramatic background to the combed decoration. Shellac dries fast, within half an hour or so, making a convenient metallic finish. It should be brushed on with the grain, rapidly but as evenly as possible, till the wood is covered. Let dry hard, about one hour.

III. COMBING GLAZE

To create a combed finish that would contrast well with the gilt base a richly coloured glaze was mixed, using alizarin crimson, burnt umber, and a little burnt sienna, dissolved in white spirit, then thickened with proprietary transparent oil glaze to a thin cream consistency. This was brushed over the gilt surfaces of the box, one facet at a time, and left to 'set up' for a moment or two, before using the rubber graining comb to create a regular pattern of combed squares, as shown, combing horizontally for one square, vertically for the next. A chequer-board like this does not need to be mathematically accurate; the pattern is the important part.

IV. FINISHING

Combing, as the word implies, simply means pulling the rubber comb teeth through the transparent glaze colour, to create stripes. As shown here, these look attractive, when regular basketweave checks are interrupted here and there by slightly wilder, rippled sections, made very easily by wobbling the comb as you pull it through the glaze. Glazes of this sort remain workable for approximately fifteen minutes to half an hour (depending on the temperature) so there is time to play around, try one effect after another, knowing the glaze can be brushed out smooth again if you are not satisfied. A finish like this does not have to be varnished, unless it will get hard wear.

CRACKLE GLAZE

HOW TO CRACK 'CRACKLE'

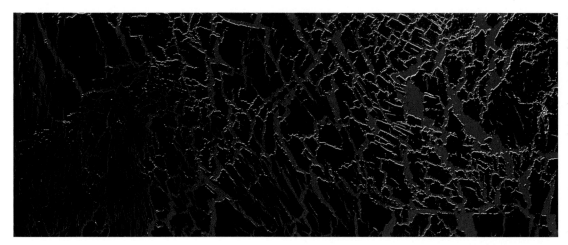

Crackle glaze is a sticky preparation which chemically reproduces the 'alligatoring' that develops where two elements in a paint finish dry at a different rate and a network of cracks splits up the top coat. This happens more commonly with old varnishes than paint, and it seems highly likely that the first attempt to produce the effect to order was made by the fakers of paintings by the Old Masters, who realized how effectively a fine *craquelure* cobwebbing of the varnish on a painting lent a convincing patina of age. A French firm of artists' suppliers markets a system that successfully counterfeits the fine crackle seen on old paintings and other varnished objects. Several manufacturers of small painted objects have used this to give subtle surface interest, enhanced by rubbing in an antiquing glaze, but the system is expensive and requires careful timing and handling for success.

The crackled effects fashionable among the newer furniture designers are altogether different, producing crude and dramatic surface crazing more like a dried-up river bed than the fine cobwebby effect described above. The trend is to exploit the exciting, random pattern of the crackle by using strong, contrasting paint colours on top of each other with the glaze sandwiched between so that the colour beneath 'grins' through surface cracks, creating an interesting two tone effect.

Crackle glaze is activated by contact with water, which dictates the use of water-based emulsion paints. The process needs to be rehearsed once or

Left: The interesting shapes and clean lines of three old metal boxes make a good foil for the striking effect created by crackle glazing between two contrasting layers of matt emulsion colour. Some painters use this effect on old furniture to suggest age. It combines well with other strong, folksy effects like combing, spattering and marbling. It is essential to seal crackled surfaces with varnish. A gloss varnish sets off dark colours admirably, while a matt varnish looks more 'antique'.

twice to understand how to use it with confidence and success, but once the principle is grasped it is a great deal faster than the oil-based *craquelure* and the results are bold and decorative in a very contemporary idiom – well suited to dramatizing simple pieces and interesting shapes, whether brand new unit furniture in a combination of wood and MDF or junk finds like the attractive 19th-century metal hat boxes and deed boxes used in our photographs. The charm of crackle glaze is that the effect happens automatically, within seconds, under one's astonished eyes. Controlling the results to a certain extent, so that the cracks are varied and impressive and the surface colour is sufficiently opaque, is the part that may require some rehearsal. One of the advantages of the water-based system is that if a trial run goes wrong, both the top coat and the crackle glaze can be washed off with a sponge and another attempt made almost immediately.

Crackle glaze is available in bulk quantities from specialist shops, although this is an expensive way of buying it unless you plan to use it on a grand, commercial scale. House Style Crackle Glaze Kits supply glaze and co-ordinated paint colours in domestic quantities.

The most exciting crackling usually results from using a dark colour over a bright one, like our black on scarlet. It works much better than light on dark and gives more professional-looking results.

MATERIALS

Acrylic primer or red oxide metal primer; contrasting matt emulsion colours in 500ml sizes; 500ml of crackle glaze; standard decorators' brush, in 2 inch/5cm or 2½ inch/6cm widths; wire wool; clear gloss or semi-gloss polyurethane varnish and varnish brush.

METHOD

Prime the surfaces with acrylic primer or red oxide metal primer before applying the base coat. Give all surfaces one or two coats of the matt emulsion colour chosen for the base coat (the colour should be opaque). Smooth the surfaces over lightly, using wire wool, and dust free of wire particles.

Apply crackle glaze over the base colour, using a standard decorators' brush and brushing the glaze out thinly (this makes for bigger cracks). The glaze is awkward stuff to brush out evenly and thinly because of its oddly sticky consistency, like thin grainy honey, but cracks only form on the top coat where it comes into contact with the glaze, so it is important that this transparent glaze covers the entire surface. Check by holding the piece up to the window – the glazed surface is shiny. On vertical surfaces even brushing is still more important, because you want to avoid drips and runs (the effect known as 'curtaining'). If the piece is small enough, it is simpler to move it about so that each facet or surface is horizontal while you apply the glaze. Leave the glaze to dry thoroughly; overnight is about right, though this can be speeded up by using a hairdryer or standing the piece in a warm place.

The skill in crackle glazing comes in applying the top coat evenly and quickly to give well-defined crackling. If you rehearse this on a board you will find that cracks begin to appear within seconds of applying the top coat of matt emulsion over the glaze. They are caused by the water in the emulsion coming into contact with the water-activated glaze and the difficulty is that while this process is happening the glaze is highly volatile; do not keep brushing out over the same spot or you will find it all sliding about messily. You have only about 10 seconds after putting on one brushstroke of top

Above: A close-up shows the variations in scale which can be achieved with crackle effects. The black box surface was painted in a horizontal position, hence the evenness of the surface crazing. The white box, painted on the vertical, shows larger cracks where the paint has begun slipping down a little. This is the way to get dramatic effects, but it is more chancy.

colour in which you can re-brush to even the colour, or overlap a second stroke over the first without dislodging the paint. Part of the secret is getting the right amount of paint on your brush; there should be enough to cover one strip from edge to edge but not so much you drop a great blob as you begin brushing. The aim is to paint the surface a strip at a time, each strip slightly overlapping the one before. If you have reason to think the last strip of paint has reached the volatile stage, the solution is to leave a thin space before applying the next brushload. These 'skips' can be gone over separately after the top coat has dried, using a fine brush and a light touch.

It is easier to control the crackle glazing results on a horizontal surface so wherever possible tackle one facet of a piece at a time, turning it to lie horizontal. Dry thoroughly (use a hairdryer) before moving it round. If you have to paint vertical surfaces (doors and windowframes, for instance) go easy on the top coat and do not overload the brush; once the glaze starts reacting any thick patches of paint on vertical surfaces tend to start sliding down. (This can of course be used as part of a dramatic effect; it depends what you are aiming for.)

Practice beforehand will show you how to achieve a good effect; it is worth persevering because results can be spectacular. The crackling itself is exciting to watch. Within seconds a newly applied paint surface begins crazing, finely at first, then rapidly opening up; this goes on, with the cracks continuing to expand, until the surface is dry. Then go back and do any neatening up needed, filling in 'skips' and tidying up corners and edges.

Crackle-glazed pieces must be varnished, preferably with two coats. (If an unvarnished surface had water spilled on it the paint would come off.) An antiquing glaze can be rubbed over the varnished finish to emphasize the crackle.

CRACKLE GLAZE – STEP BY STEP

I. PREPARATION

Victorian metal hat-boxes like this are fun to paint, and look highly decorative crackled in various colourways. The original painted finish may be battered, but under a crackled finish no one will know. However it is worth rubbing them down with medium grade sandpaper to remove any loose, flaky paint. Rusty metal needs more serious attention to prevent the rust working away underneath the new paint. An application of rust remover, followed by scouring with medium grade wire wool, will clean off loose rust and this can be sealed in with metal primer.

II. BASE PAINTING

Two coats of scarlet matt emulsion have been applied over a coat of red oxide metal primer to give an opaque, solid red base for the crackling. Don't forget to paint the base as well as the top and sides of the box; there is something half-hearted as well as unprofessional about items painted only on the obviously visible surfaces. Using the same red base colour over the interior of the box adds to the pleasure of opening it. Other colour combinations which work well with the crackle glaze are dark blue over emerald green, dark green over burnt sienna, blue-green over barn red.

III. CRACKLING

Once the red base is dry, a coat of crackle glaze is brushed over the entire surface to be crackled, brushing the slightly sticky glaze out quite thinly and evenly. On a small item like this box the glaze will hold well on the vertical surfaces, even after the crackling has started. On larger pieces it pays off in the long run to shift the piece round so that you are always working on a horizontal surface. This has been found to give the best crackle. Impatient people can use a hairdryer to hurry these operations along. The direction you brush on the glaze determines the crackle formation; brushing every which way gives the most random crackle.

IV. FINISHING

The black coat has been brushed rapidly over the dry crackle glaze, using enough paint on the brush to cover a strip at a time, and working fast so that a second strip of black slightly overlaps the first before that one starts cracking up. Once the crackle appears the new paint should not be touched till dry, because till then it remains volatile, and apt to slide about. If you have been obliged to leave gaps between strips of top coat, the solution is to fill these in after the top coat has dried. Here a shiny gloss varnish is being applied to seal the crackling (essential) and enhance the effect.

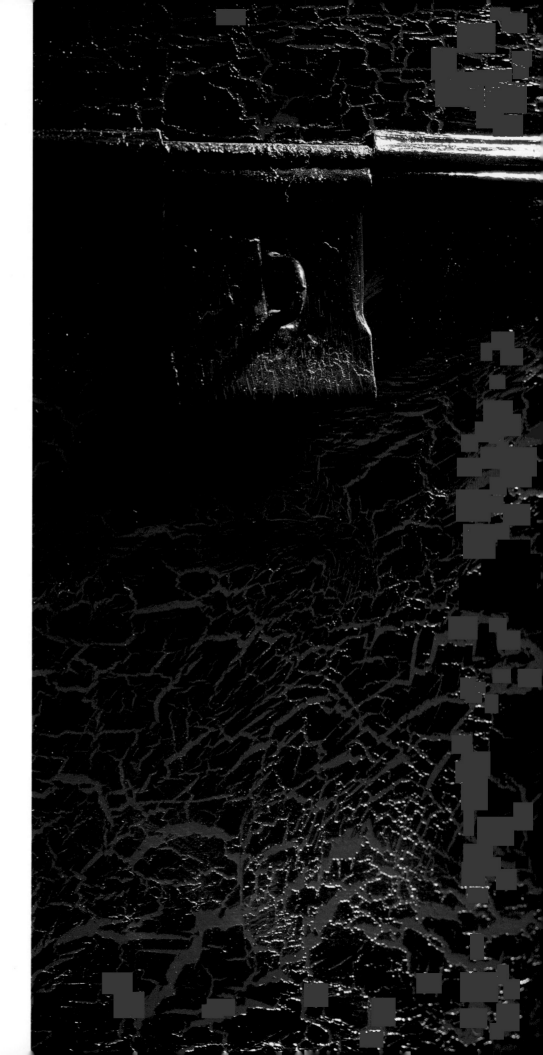

Right: Crackle glaze looks exceptionally smart done in strong, contrasting colours, here black on scarlet, shinily varnished for extra 'oomph'. Crackle glaze can be used successfully on other materials besides metal; wood, MDF, even plastic.

FAUX LACQUER

GLOSS OVER A JUNK TABLE

The opulent gloss, like the sheen on a well-groomed thoroughbred's coat, of an oil-based paint finish rubbed and varnished to an immaculate shine has a striking presence in an interior scheme. It was first recognized in the shape of the simpler Japanese lacquer which became popular around the turn of this century and was developed by designers of the Art Deco movement of the 1920s (notably Eileen Gray and the Frenchman Jean Dunand) into a soberly luxurious effect which gave an air of great quality to the streamlined furniture shapes of the period. Gray and Dunand used the true Oriental lacquer for their effects, it must be said, but before long competent tradesmen and finishers were producing sleek imitations using Western materials and methods which had the surface shine, if not the subtle depth of colour, of the Oriental process. The distinguishing feature of *faux* lacquer work of this sort is its austerity; with a few exceptions, the splendidly glossy paint finish was decoration enough.

Faux lacquer, because it involves the use of slow-drying oil-based paint, together with many finishing coats of varnish, is one of the more patient and labour-intensive transformations considered here. On the other hand, finishes that take longer to complete tend to last considerably longer, and mellow pleasingly with use. *Faux* lacquer would be an ideal choice for an attractive Deco item with a cleancut period shape yet made of ugly or uninteresting wood, or surfaced in wood veneer, immediately upgrading its appearance and possible resale value. Likewise, for anyone with a bit of time

Left: The mellow gleam of a faux *lacquer finish in bright red picks up the shine of a pretty eastern box, and the patina of old mahogany. A deep shine like this, achieved by layers of clear varnish and patient smoothing with wet-and-dry paper, looks very classy even on a nothing-special junk shop piece like this little table.*

Left: Deep shine and bright colour make their own statement.

FAUX LACQUER – STEP BY STEP

I. PREPARATION

The table in its original state, but with the dark varnish stain fiercely rubbed back to bare wood. A little lingering stain as seen here is not a problem, but if there is a lot of it and you are painting over in a pale colour, it is sensible to paint first with a sealing aluminium primer, which prevents old stain (aniline based) seeping through new paint layers. A power sander saves muscle power on jobs like this, but it is usually a good idea to finish by hand to smooth it further.

II. BASE COAT

Here the table has had its first coat of acrylic primer. Two, even three coats are needed, depending on the original surface, to create as smooth and even a finish as possible. High shine effects like this one tend to blow up any defects in the surface, and make them more obvious. Use standard filler to fill any cracks, dents, chips, etc. after the first coat of primer, when they will show up better. After the second coat use fine filler to fill small cracks, pits, tiny flaws. Rub down both times and seal over with a dab more primer.

III. PAINTING COLOUR

The table has now been given three coats of bright red eggshell paint, rubbed down lightly when dry, in between, and it looks jolly but unsubtle, like a pillar box. For suggestions as to other colours for lacquering see the section on lacquer and japanned furniture on page 11. On the whole strong vivid colours, or subtle pastels, look best, as of course does black, or the deep brownish black seen on many oriental lacquer wares.

IV. FINISHING

Before receiving its glassy layers of clear varnish, the vivid red surface was softened by painting over and ragging off a smoky coloured thin oil glaze, to take the glare off the red and give a hint of Oriental inscrutability, shadowiness. A quick 'scumble' like this is a useful way of 'knocking back' overly bright colours. The snag is that it needs to be left to dry out thoroughly before applying the layers of varnish. Varnish is applied thinned to start with, and with a fine bristled varnish brush, to give as smooth a surface as possible. Wet-and-dry rubbing takes care of any remaining flaws.

MARBLING
MARBLING MAPPED OUT

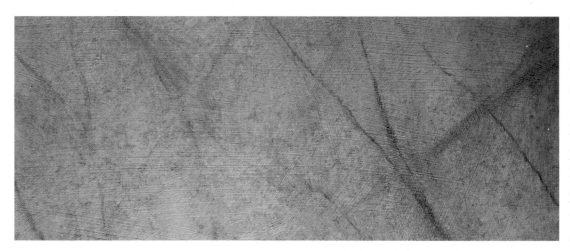

Marbling has been used since Roman times to imitate in paint the streakings and colouring of real fossil stone on lesser materials such as plaster, wood and slate. Like real marble, the painted variety has tended to be associated with architectural elements – cornices, pilasters, dados – and this is how it was first introduced as a decorative element in painted furniture. During the late 17th century, when marbling was fashionable all over Europe, it began to appear on the cornices, pediments and other architectural features on the monumental furniture that was then fashionable. Marbling was always important in church decoration, particularly in the northern countries where wood was a great deal cheaper and more accessible than real marble, and marbled altars, columns, and pulpits, such as one finds throughout northern Europe, may well have been the inspiration behind the use of marbling on the cornice and base of so many massive provincial cupboards, dressers and bureaux.

If upper-class furniture used marbling with discretion, for cornices and table tops, the folk painters felt no such inhibitions. They seized on its striking decorative potential and used it freely, combined with areas of plain colour or with other painted decoration, wherever they felt it would look impressive, from door panels to chair legs, without regard for appropriateness. But then their ignorance of real marble was such that marbling in their various traditions became something abstract, a colourful melange of dots, dashes and zigzags which could be brushed in rapidly, gave

Left: Who says marbling need look showy or pretentious? This bevy of chairs shows marbling in a lighter, rustic mood, its wisps of colour and delicate veining doing wonders for simple wooden frames, and bringing unexpected freshness to four quite ordinary chairs. Marbled rush-seated chairs, usually in blue on white, survive from the 18th century in Sweden. We show four colourways here, as supplied by House Style's Marbling Kits.

an air of importance, and made their boldly decorated furniture even more eye-catching. A lot of the painted marbling on European and American provincial furniture is difficult to recognize for what it is or aspires to be – i.e., painted imitation of stone markings; it may be spotted like a leopard, or striped like a tiger, in non-naturalistic colours. The so-called 'clouds marbling' of the Swedish province Hallingdal uses the convention of a cupid's bow shape traced in white on a dark blue background. Verisimilitude was the last thing on anyone's mind; what mattered to the painters was that this sort of decorative work went quickly, while what counted with the clients was that it looked impressive.

Serious *trompe l'oeil* marbling sometimes appears on the more expensive furniture, most often disguising the wooden tops of painted tables and commodes. The showier types of marble tended to be imitated here, the dark greens and richly mottled reds, purples and yellows rather than the lightly streaked, mainly grey carrara which is probably the most commonly used variety in the world. Of course a strong part of the appeal of *faux* finishes is that cost limits do not operate as they would normally; it may cost no more to have the most extravagant marble, such as onyx, imitated than the cheaper ones.

Marbling today is generally architectural, used on cornices, skirtings, fireplaces, and sometimes dados, in the 17th-century manner. It is used less than it might be on painted furniture, which is a pity, because this is often where it looks original and charming. One reason for this may be that amateur painters, especially beginners, are intimidated by the marbling technique, with its glazes and feathers and complex markings and colours. The 'veining', especially, is a problem. To get round this, and demonstrate that marbling can be used with success by beginners, we have marbled four rush-seated countrified chairs

Above: This detail shows two other marbling colourways in greater detail, the predominantly Yellow Siena, and the rose-tinted Pink Granite. One kit is ample to paint four chairs, with enough left over to marble a table to match.

from kits. House Style Marbling Kits feature one aid specially designed to encourage novices – veining 'maps', three to a kit, which allow veining patterns to be traced off, sponged over, then redrawn with feather and veining medium without trepidation. The kits come in the four colourways shown, and also include co-ordinated marbling colours and detailed instructions.

MATERIALS

1 litre vinyl silk emulsion; House Style Marbling Kit in Blue Rococo, Pink Granite, Grey Carrara and Yellow Siena. Contents include natural sponge, goose feather, two marbling colours, veining medium and three veining maps; soft and hard lead pencils; Craig and Rose Extra Pale Dead Flat varnish or clear eggshell varnish for slight sheen; varnish brush; fine grade wire wool.

METHOD

Furniture should be primed and painted with two coats of off-white vinyl silk emulsion. Standard white vinyl silk emulsion can be 'dirtied' or softened by simply mixing in a little yellow ochre and raw umber tinting agent, artists' acrylic tube colour, commercial stainers or gouache colour.

Carbon paper to trace off the veining would have been awkward to fit round chair legs, so we used soft lead pencil to scribble over the back of the maps. Re-drawing on the right side, using a hard pencil point, leaves a clear enough impression of the patterns to work from; go over lightly with pencil if necessary to make it clearer and also to join up veining here and there around the legs. Obviously veining flows much more readily over flat surfaces, like table tops and door panels; on the other hand it looks unexpected and pretty decorating chairs like these, so the extra work was justified. Using the first marble colour

and the natural sponge, a pale neutral shade was sponged in loose drifts over most of the surface, including the pencilled veining (the marbling colours are transparent so the veins show through). Over this the second marbling colour was sponged more densely, forming clusters, but over less of the total surface. Using the varnish brush bristle tips, gently 'soften' the colours to smooth out some of the spottiness caused by sponging, and create areas of clear transparent colour. With the tip of the feather dripped in veining medium the pencilled veining was redrawn, using a loose-wristed, almost rippling action which gives the maximum variety to the strokes, suggesting the diversity of natural veining. (Practice with the feather on a board or paper first if you feel clumsy with it.)

The next step, the 'softening' of the veins, is what makes painted marble look convincing. Using the tips of the varnish brush bristles, very gently blur and smudge the veins, whisking the tips this way and that for variety. The veining medium stays malleable for up to half an hour so there are opportunities for second thoughts, and softening can be left to the end of marbling a surface instead of being done as you go along.

Leave the piece to dry thoroughly at this stage, so the colours settle and you get a break from it. On going back you'll usually find the first effort too timid, so this is the point to strengthen colours and drift rhythms, and to emphasize the veining more boldly here and there. Once again soften the veins, allow to dry, then apply two coats of varnish or, as professionals prefer, with one coat of gloss followed by one coat of matt varnish, which is supposed to give depth and slight lustre with the strength of gloss protection. Rub over the varnish very lightly with wire wool when dry to remove any grit, dust, hairs and so on. The surfaces can be further waxed and polished for a softer sheen, typical of older marble.

MARBLING – STEP BY STEP

I. PREPARATION

The chair shown here has been primed, with acrylic primer, filled and rubbed down, and then given two coats of white vinyl silk emulsion. Matt emulsion can be substituted successfully, if you want a no-sheen finish, though this is less characteristic of marbling. On a matt base the marbling tends to be stronger, and folksier looking. Whatever white emulsion is used it is usually a good idea to 'dirty' it a little by mixing in a small amount of yellow ochre and raw umber. This takes off the whiter than white brightness.

II. MAPPING THE VEINS

Three veining maps, supplied with House Style kits, make veining a simple business, a fact beginners find encouraging. To use the maps scribble over the back of the paper with soft lead pencil, then trace off over the right side on to the surface. On a tricky shape like a chair, with its round legs and small surfaces, it may be easier to cut the maps into smaller pieces for handling. Take a photocopy first and then you won't have lost the use of your map on future projects.

III. APPLYING COLOURS

The kits provide a natural sponge and two transparent marbling colours, smoky grey and blue. The chair has been sponged over loosely with both, allowing a little drying time between, and the colour has been smoothed out and softened by gentle working over with the brush tips. Some white ground colour should be left showing with the Blue Rococo effect, and the blue sponged colour should sometimes be softened over the smoky grey and sometimes teased out to transparency on its own.

IV. VEINING AND VARNISHING

The final step is the one that sharpens up the effect and pulls it all together. Using the goosefeather supplied, as shown on the right, and the veining medium (here a deep blue) re-draw in veining following the pencilled lines which show through the transparent sponging colours. Use the feather in a loose, even limp-wristed fashion, letting the feather lead you and make its own irregular marks, lighter in some places, broken in others. The medium stays workable for some time, at least twenty minutes. Use brush tips again to soften and blur the veins, brushing with, across, then diagonally. Varnish when dry to protect.

Right: Marbled in Blue Rococo, this chair would look perfectly at home in a typically Gustavian decor, with light pearl grey woodwork, scrubbed floors and snowy muslin curtains.

MARQUETRY

A PINE BOX GOES UPMARKET

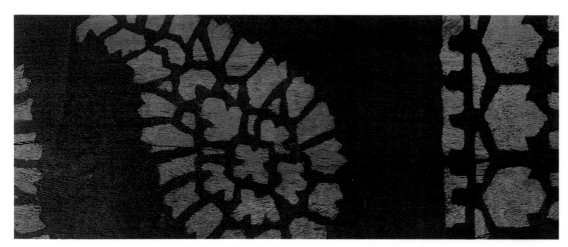

Real marquetry is a decorative jigsaw, using shapes cut out of variously coloured and figured wood veneers, fitted together to make up a pattern or image which is glued under pressure on to a carcass, usually of softwood. Dutch cabinet-makers of the 17th century were especially skilful at creating furniture with elaborate marquetry surfaces; these pieces have mellowed to a wonderful tawny richness of colouring over the centuries and are coveted examples of their period. As well as furniture, marquetry has been used occasionally on doors, shutters and other architectural fittings to give an effect of Oriental lavishness and an intensely decorative effect.

Marquetry is one of the easier traditional decorative processes to imitate, using stencils and wood stains over bare wood or stencils and wood-coloured paints over painted wood. The latter may be simpler and quicker if the alternative involves massive stripping work on old paint, but the illusion is more complete when the technique is applied on bare wood, because the visibility of the grain adds to the authenticity and richness of the effect. The late Geoffrey Bennison, one of the most creative post-war decorators, sometimes used stencilled marquetry combined with graining over the entire woodwork of a period room. Combined with the grandly faded fabrics he designed and the darker atmospheric colours he favoured, the overall effect was sumptuous and original, especially suited to late 19th-century interiors.

Left: Sometimes the simplest ideas give the most spectacular results through some unobvious sleight-of-hand. You wonder why you never thought of that before. Here a straightforward use of masking fluid and a stencil, plus wood stain, adds up to a truly sumptuous looking decorative finish, which we have called faux *marquetry.*

However, as our marquetry box shows, there is no need to be so ambitious to get a lot of pleasure from owning a piece in the warm tawny tones of '*faux* marquetry'. Bennison had stencils made in imitation of traditional marquetry patterns, which tend to be complex and busy, almost filigree, but this again was perfectionist. Any bold and handsome stencil motif will give a strongly decorative effect. The one shown, based on the paisley leaf or feather, is taken from the Paintability range of stencil kits, which gives several borders as well as spot motifs. There are so many commercial stencils to choose from today that it should be easy to find a design that suits your taste and your furniture, from filigree florals to geometric patterns.

Our *faux* marquetry example stays within the 'simple' brief in the sense that it uses only one stain colour, in contrast to the original blondwood. However, it would be quite possible to introduce more stain colours to a design, either by painting them in by hand with a fine brush and a selection of stains (these come in dozens of wood shades, from black to blond) or by extending the masking off principle, but in reverse, so that the masking fluid protects the previously stained surfaces you do not want coloured again. Outlining the marquetry shapes with a fine line of black Indian ink, or with a Rotring pen, will make a complex marquetry design look even more like the real thing. This is only worth doing in the case of a small, exquisite object which will be inspected closely because on a larger scale item the value of this sort of painstaking finishing touch is much reduced.

MATERIALS

Masking fluid (available from artists' suppliers); foam decorators' sponge; small tin of spirit-based wood stain in mid-oak shade; stencils; masking tape; clear gloss polyurethane varnish and varnish brush; fine grade wire wool; plastic gloves.

METHOD

Strip off wax, varnish or French polish (see stripping techniques on page 24) to leave the wood clean and bare. Because the charming brass-bound box in our pictures was made of such a mellow pine, we used that as the base colour. If your base is a whitewood, not pretty enough to look good unadorned, it is a simple extra process to begin by staining the entire piece in a golden tone of wood stain. After it is dry the procedure is exactly the same.

Work out the best use of stencils for your particular item (make a sketch to guide yourself if the arrangement is at all complicated). Fix the stencils with masking tape to hold them steady during use. Use the foam sponge to apply masking fluid through the stencils on to the bare or stained wood. This looks milky at first but dries transparent, so you will need to hold the piece up to the light to make sure where you have stencilled. When this has been completed, use the sponge or a clean rag to swab wood stain over the entire surface, first going across, then with, the grain. Repeat until you have the depth of colour you want. Leave to dry. Then rub gently with your fingers at the areas stencilled with masking fluid and you will find the masking fluid peels off bit by bit, leaving blond designs 'inlaid' into dark surrounding wood. This looks stunningly effective left just as it is, but you might wish to add more colours at this stage. If you look at an antique marquetry piece you will find as many as half a dozen tones used, including black and, sometimes, green. These could be brushed in carefully now, before final varnishing. Use small, soft artists' brushes and take care not to flood the shape you are colouring in with stain or it may seep over its boundaries and blur your crisp pattern. This is quicker than masking off on small areas. Outlining with a Rotring pen (see penwork on page 82) or a dip pen and Indian

Left: The charm of this finish is that it makes use of the texture of the wood itself, both bare and stained. This lends enormous warmth and character to the decorative patterning. A bold stencil design like this one by Paintability, called The Indian Kitchen, creates a strong, eyecatching effect; for a softer look, you could use a fine cut, all-over type of stencil, or even cut your own in imitation of old Dutch marquetry.

ink is painstaking but satisfying, because it sharpens up designs so effectively and mimics the real thing.

A similar marquetry effect could be obtained over painted surfaces, using transparent oil glaze tinted in wood colours. The base should be ivory white eggshell. Apply a golden tinted glaze overall (yellow ochre, raw sienna, a touch of raw umber), to simulate a pale wood base like pine or sycamore. Brush out thinly, and rag over lightly to give it a little texture. Leave to dry hard. Stencil with masking fluid as already described. Then

re-glaze overall using a glaze tinted a cool walnut brown (burnt umber, raw sienna, a dot of black) or a rich mahogany (burnt umber, a little vermilion and alizarin crimson, a dot of black). This should be dragged to make grain-type markings by pulling using a 2 inch/5cm brush firmly through the wet glaze to leave stripes. Dragging should always imitate the way the grain lies on the wood beneath, with horizontal grain and vertical grain butting up at right angles. Masking tape is helpful here. Use to delimit a dragged section, peeling off when glaze dries and then dragging in the opposite direction.

When your marquetry, whether stained or painted, is finished and thoroughly dry (this will take days using glazes) varnish over with two coats of clear gloss polyurethane to suggest the gleam of polished wood. Use soft wire wool, rubbing in a circular movement, to dim the shine to a silky sheen. A light waxing and buffing with furniture polish can be tried too, for a natural-looking wood sheen.

Left: A sliver of box and marquetry shows just how beat up the box had become, peppered with upholstery tacks, and what a difference in colour there is between the bare and stained wood.

MARQUETRY – STEP BY STEP

I. PREPARATION

The box unadorned, an attractive looking piece in its own right, with its brass banding and pretty tawny pine. Note the dovetailing at corners, always the mark of a well-made piece because it makes a much stronger join than pins and glue. It would have been perfectionist to fill the tack holes with plastic wood, and rub them level before decorating the box, but this sort of attention is always optional, depending on the value of the piece and how much time you can spare.

II. NEGATIVE STENCILLING

One of the pre-cut stencils from the Paintability Indian Kitchen set, has been taped in place on the box with masking tape. Using masking fluid, the pattern was sponged through the stencil cut-outs. The rest of the design was carried out the same way. Just how you arrange the stencils is the personal bit, but using them to echo the lines of a piece – up the legs, across the front, filling a panel or table top – usually works best. Masking fluid goes clear as it dries, visible by its shine only.

III. STAINING

Having stencilled in negative over the whole box, a mid oak wood stain was swabbed over the whole box. We used a big brush, but you could also use a sponge or rag. Keep repeating this till the colour is as deep as you want it. Keep the stain fairly even – you don't want dark patches cropping up; the colour usually takes two or three applications to reach full intensity. The stencilled areas will register, as here, as dark designs.

IV. MARQUETRY REVEALED

The marquetry revealed, in all its bold impact, set in a rich brown surround. To do this, you leave the stain to dry for the stated time. Remove the masking fluid by gently rubbing with your fingertips. You will find it peels away quite easily, leaving perfectly clear negative prints. As I have suggested, a further elaboration could be to outline the shapes in pen and ink – Indian ink – or use a Rotring pen. This undoubtedly furthers the illusion of inlay work, though you may feel that the simple contrast shown here is exciting enough as it stands.

PENWORK

DOODLING FOR REAL WITH PENWORK

Penwork decoration is really doodling made deliberate, using pen and ink to inscribe fine black line ornament on to pale painted surfaces, or one of the paler toned woods. The designs used can be traced off old examples or, of course, invented by yourself. From a distance a lot of penwork looks like decoratively carved ivory, or that traditional work on whale tooth and whale bone called 'scrimshaw'. Penwork is a neat – and cheap – way of arriving at a lavish effect with just a few materials, and it can transform a simple item like the junk mirror frame shown here into something highly covetable.

Unless you are confident and skilful enough at drawing to try freehand penwork, you will need to provide yourself first with a selection of attractive, suitable subjects. Elements that combine well are ornamental borders in different widths, open-work designs for covering background areas, and a selection of graceful traditional motifs such as bouquets, bows, garlands, cherubs, 'trophies' and so forth to use centrally. You can work from old drawings (especially pen and ink drawings of course) but on the whole, old engravings and etchings make the best design inspiration for penwork, which tends to look most impressive when the surface is quite densely and finely worked – at least this seems to have been the view of the 18th and 19th-century penworkers, many of them amateurs, who specialized in copying from engravings of classical scenes, or ones based on famous paintings. The top and sides of a wooden workbox, for instance, might be

Left: Thinking ink, as decoration, using a nifty drawing pen, on a pale coloured base, has turned this modest little mirror into a strikingly attractive and original piece. This is a formula with immense potential. Not new, it was popular in the 18th century. Not fast, because any doodling takes time, but it is the sort of effect that sells itself in a shop window.

penworked with mythological scenes faithfully copied from engravings *aprés* Claude Lorrain or Nicolas Poussin. Each little panel would be enclosed in a frame of penworked ornament, usually scrolling foliage in the classical manner. Famous views and monuments, flower pieces, naval battles and scenes of rustic life were all popular themes for penworking, usually as little 'vignettes' on boxes, firescreens, tea caddies, papier mâché trays and other small items. This work was usually done in black on white, but one sometimes sees penwork in sepia, or 'sanguine' (brown-red) ink over white.

Used to decorate larger pieces, like the workboxes on stands, cabinets and *etagères* which seem to have been such popular items under the Regency, penwork became bolder, the scale of the ornament larger and plain black backgrounds provided a strong contrast which allowed the ornament to be 'read' at a distance. Collecting suitable subjects of different shapes and sizes must have been a problem in the days before photocopying machines made instant copying, and enlarging or reducing the size of the original, a perfectly simple procedure. Artistic amateurs kept sketchbooks, for reference as well as experiment; probably they copied prints and engravings into them and then used these to work from.

Penwork takes a while to do, though modern pens make it speedier than before. It is best to begin on something quite small and light, for example a tray or box or frame as here, where a little penwork goes further, decoratively speaking, and the elegant work visibly growing under your hands will encourage you to persevere adding a bit more as and when you have time.

MATERIALS

0.5mm Rotring drawing pen with black ink cartridge; rough sandpaper; off-white matt emulsion in matchpot size (200ml); fine-grade wire wool; tracing and carbon paper; soft lead pencil and pencil sharpener; masking tape; clear matt or semi-gloss polyurethane varnish and varnish brush.

METHOD

The wooden mirror frame was sanded hard with rough sandpaper to remove most of its former varnish and given one coat of acrylic primer and two coats of off-white matt emulsion to build up an opaquely white surface like paper. The smoother the surface the easier it is to keep up a flowing line with your pen. The paint was smoothed by gentle rubbing over with fine wire wool. Serious cracks and dents should be filled and rubbed smooth between emulsion coats. Avoid oak, or wood with a ridgy grain or open grain, because these will be difficult to draw on.

Ornamental bands for the decoration were traced from one of the many books of ornament currently available. The choice was dictated by the shape of the frame – long, narrow bands for the sides, rectangular shapes for top and bottom. Varying the intensity of the pattern and using a lot of small chequers in the background adds up to a rich but crisp effect which reads well at a distance. The finished mirror looks like something which would not be out of place in a Florentine painting. Note too how simple rosettes have been used to balance the motifs on the top of the frame and fill in awkward leftover spaces.

Because the patterns were relatively straightforward, carbon paper was dispensed with for the tracing off process to save time and fiddling about. Instead, the designs were traced out of the source book using architects' tracing paper. The back of the paper was heavily scribbled over with soft lead pencil. Then the designs were turned right way round, fixed in place with tabs

Left: A close-up shows the penworked design in greater detail. Though it looks impressive, the whole thing was traced out of a book of ornament. The contrast of fine line and bold checks is specially effective.

of masking tape and redrawn on the right side. This leaves a clear enough impression to work from and it makes locating the patterns accurately much easier than if a sheet of carbon was sandwiched between blocking off the view, so to speak.

It is always a little alarming to launch off with the ink, which looks so permanent, though slips and mistakes can be whited out again. A few minutes' doodling with the Rotring will give you the feel of its superfine tip, and make you keen to begin.

Once you are started it is plain sailing – you simply redraw over the traced outlines using the Rotring, completing one section at a time. Being cartridge-fed, the pen keeps up a continuous flow instead of needing to be dipped continuously, which saves time. The ink is not so tough or glossy as Indian ink, and needs sealing with varnish, but on a smooth, well-prepared finished it gives an elegant, clear line. Use Indian ink and a fine brush to fill in larger background areas in black. Two coats of ink may be needed for total blackness.

Varnish the completed work with at least one coat of varnish to seal and give an ivory-like sheen. If you prefer a mellower tint to your ivory, a coat of thinned orange shellac between varnish coats will supply this. Alternatively, rub a little tan boot polish over the final finish, and polish off with soft rags to leave just the hint of a tint.

PENWORK – STEP BY STEP

I. PREPARATION

This is how the mirror looked after its softwood frame had been energetically sanded back to remove old varnish and stain, and prepare the surface for an ivory white undercoat, all in the same operation. Penwork was always supposed to mimic carved ivory, as in traditional Indian furniture and knick-knacks, so the base colour should shade off in that direction. Also, to further suggest the smoothness of ivory, it matters that cracks are filled, chips levelled off and so forth. Use fine filler, fill 'proud' above base level, let dry, then sand smooth.

II. BASE COATING

The frame was carefully prepared, using first one coat of acrylic primer, which fills as well as giving paint something to grip on to. Then two coats of ivory white matt emulsion were brushed over the whole surface. If you don't have ivory white, mix a little raw sienna, ochre or raw umber into plain white – not a tinful. For a frame this size, one teacupful will be enough. An alternative route to the mellow white of old ivory is to slap on bright white base coat, but finish with a warm varnish, like orange shellac.

III. TRACING OFF PATTERNS

The artist at work, sneakily tracing appropriate motifs and emblems out of one of the many books of printed ornament now on the market. As with stencils, the artwork may be a steal, but how you put motifs together to fit your space is what gives the inimitable personal touch. Don't overlook the possibilities of working initials, copperplate messages, little personal allusions, into this sort of piece. It could provide a rich mine of cheap Christmas presents, which will be treasured even if they don't find their way into the Victoria and Albert Museum.

IV. VARNISHING

Could anything be more elegantly Florentine, or Lake Palace of Udaipur than the finished frame? Imagine transferring this elegance to a picture frame, or a photo frame. I don't know anyone who would not respond to this vivid, striking, and supremely effective example of decorativeness pure and simple. See the Masterclass penwork feature (page 126) for further suggestions. Your inclinations may run to the miniature, or the full-blown, but anyone who likes doodling has it made with this finish. Give it one or two (depending on what it is and the wear it receives) coats of varnish, or orange shellac plus varnish.

Right: Anyone can scribble in simple basketweave shapes and sun-in-glory emblems like those shown here, especially when the design has been traced off on to the surface previously, and the reference for it is at your elbow.

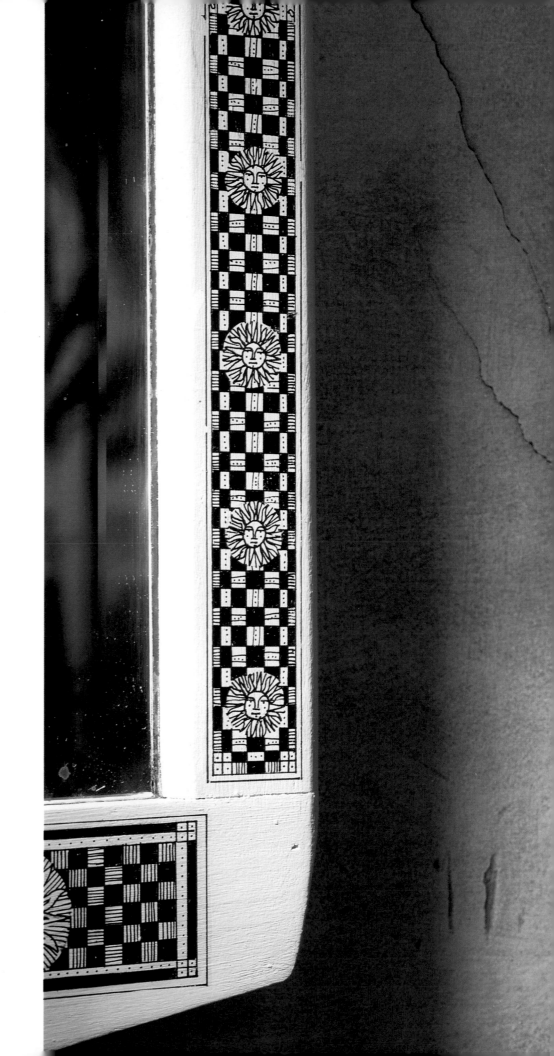

VERDIGRIS
THE AGEING TREND

The natural blue-green patination of noble materials like bronze and copper which occurs through oxidation and exposure is readily imitated with paint, which is probably why this is currently one of the most fashionable distressed finishes with both grand interior decorators and trendy young designers. The range of verdigris colours, from pale turquoise through to an almost sulphurous blue, is handsome in itself and seems to blend equally happily into a luxurious traditional interior or a coolly minimal avant-garde one. The distressing involved gives a look of age and value even over plastics and resins, yet it is not showy or pretentious as gilding might be; and the finish looks just as good dramatizing a small wall sconce as dressing up a suite of metal garden furniture. The latter is at present extremely fashionable, and a verdigris treatment is ideal for upgrading the less impressive metals, such as aluminium and cast iron. The chalky blue-greens also look cool and pretty stippled over wickerwork.

To show the versatility of the finish, we have used it over a set of old wire baskets, bought for a song, and on a set of French cast iron garden furniture, or rather café furniture – slightly spindly chairs and tables that once were lined up outside pavement cafés and bar-restaurants all over France, now superseded by plastic. Two different methods of arriving at the verdigris look are shown; the baskets were stippled with artists' acrylic tube colours and a piece of foam over a burnt umber base; the garden suite, which has to

Left: The soft colour and weathered look of a verdigris finish on metal garden furniture settles in comfortably into an outdoor context, making a pleasant change from the conventional green or white paint. But this is a sophisticated and subtle finish which looks equally well indoors, lining a corner cupboard, giving a new look to picture frames, lamp bases and wall brackets.

Left: A curly wire basket, the sort used in France for all manner of kitchen purposes, from holding eggs to salad dressing materials, gets a new outdoorsy glamour with a verdigris finish sponged on using artists' acrylic tube colours.

VERDIGRIS – STEP BY STEP

I. PREPARATION

Get loose rust and old flaky paint off any metal or wire piece by brushing vigorously with a wire brush. Being wire a piece like this will come up quite bright, and clean. This makes all the difference to how well your decorative finish adheres. A paint finish, as the old decorative painters liked solemnly to intone, is only as good as the base and preparation, and this applies as much to modern fast paints as to the older slower drying media. Rust works away insidiously underneath.

II. PRIMING

To put a final stopper on any rust sabotage work, the basket is given a base coat of red oxide metal primer, a cheap, pleasant and useful paint which I use a fair bit as a finish, a folk type of base colour for stencils and other decoration. Here a scrap of foam sponge was used to apply the paint, much quicker on such a fiddly object than a brush. You could wrap masking tape round the handle if you are worried about getting paint on it.

III. VERDIGRIS STIPPLING

Burnt umber acrylic tube colour (here it is shown, in bulk form, in a jar, as painters prefer to buy it) is used as is to cover the entire basket, and act as a realistic dark bronze base to contrast with the ensuing blue green patination or verdigris colours. Acrylic colours dry almost immediately which explains their enormous popularity with today's decorative painting crowd. This was brushed on, but foam would have done as well.

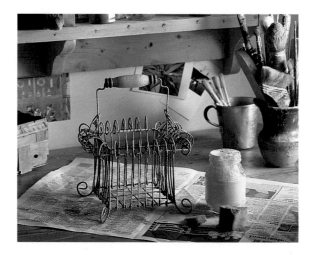

IV. HIGHLIGHTING AND VARNISHING

Using foam scraps again, acrylic colours in a vivid turquoise and emerald green, were sponged over the dark base, quite liberally, but leaving a suggestion of the dark base showing to give guts to the effect. The lighter turquoise went on first, and then emerald highlights were just touched in here and there to buzz up the effect, and make it sing out despite being no thicker than a copper wire in the first place. For outdoor use, as a plant holder perhaps, protect with two coats of varnish.

STENCILLING

CUSTOMIZED WITH COLOUR

Stencils have been one of the great discoveries for the home decorator over the past decade, a soft option for anyone looking for affordable, achievable decorative flourishes to liven their surroundings. People tend to think of stencilling as wall decoration but it looks just as good on furniture both old and new, either painted or, like the attractive pine child's desk in our pictures, unpainted. Stencilled flower sprays and borders are the customizing details that sell those fashionable painted kitchens and bathrooms that have become a status symbol from London to Los Angeles and cost an arm and a leg. Do your own customizing and the cost is peanuts. If you use pre-cut stencils and acrylic paints, stencils really are foolproof and doing them is fun; no matter how much stencilling you have done, there is something about seeing that crisp shape appear when you lift up your stencil that delights every time.

Stencils have been used for repeat patterning in all sorts of decorative processes for centuries, from painting walls and furniture to decorating pottery and precious fabrics such as the painted silks used in ceremonial Japanese kimonos. Stencilling the regularly repeating ornament would have been apprentice's work, leaving the master painter free to plan and carry out the more challenging freehand decoration. The fashion for 'powdered' ornament – i.e. motifs spaced at regular intervals on a coloured ground – led to considerable use of stencilling in the decoration of late medieval painted churches and palaces. King Henry III's favourite decorative scheme in his

Left: Stencils should be used more often to decorate furniture. This takes so much less time than stencilling walls, and gives an attractive piece like this little pine desk such a quick 'lift' visually. Here the stencils have been applied on to bare wood because the wood texture and tone was so attractive. But on a less appealing surface one would start with a few coats of colour to provide a contrasting base.

various palaces was for walls painted green and powdered with gold stars. Sadly, little evidence remains to show us what the painted and stencilled furniture of that time would have looked like, though we know from written manuals of instruction of the period that vivid, heraldic colours were preferred, lavishly trimmed with gold leaf.

With the fashion for things medieval in the mid-19th century, stencils came back into fashion for creating the gorgeous polychrome decoration that began appearing on walls and furnishings, the work of designers such as William Morris and William Burges. Burges' painted washstands, aumbries (a medieval name for cupboard), coffers and gigantic bedsteads, with their profusion of ornament in brilliant colours together with lavish inlay of semi-precious stones, must be some of the most remarkable furniture ever commissioned.

Modern taste on the whole is for a simpler, countrified effect, though latterly the craze for floral stencils in soft watercolour tones seems to be giving way to a revival of harder edged designs, with an ethnic or Art Deco feel, executed in stronger colours. The designs used to stencil our desk, for instance, were inspired by traditional flat-weave patterns used in kilim rugs. A selection of borders and spot motifs are provided in the kit, which is one of the Paintability range of pre-cut plastic stencils. The fast-drying acrylic tube colours were chosen with the mellow wood tone of the background in mind – clear but vivid blue, green and off-white. On a painted background, stronger colours would be effective. A foam pad was used for the stencilling instead of the traditional brush. This is much quicker and gives a slightly textured effect to the stencilling which is popular at the moment and suits this particular pattern. For a still more rugged texture, use a natural sponge with a 'holey' surface to apply colour.

MATERIALS

Pre-cut stencil set; artists' acrylic tube colours in blue and green; matchpot size (200ml) of matt off-white emulsion; artists' fitch brush or foam pad made by tearing a foam paint roller to pieces; clear matt or silk finish polyurethane varnish and varnish brush; masking tape; ruler; pencil; rags or kitchen paper; saucers for mixing colour.

METHOD

Spend some time working out how to make the best use of your stencils so that they complement the shape and style of your piece of furniture. Panels call for boldly centred motifs, just as rectangular tops and sides seem to yearn for outlining with stencilled borders. However, offbeat arrangements can look wonderful. Sketching possible schemes or looking through magazines on interiors may help you decide. Choose colours that echo something in the room – fabric, a rug, pictures for a together look.

Squeeze 1-2 inches/2.5-5cm of acrylic colour on to a saucer and mix in a drop of water. Adding a dot of matt emulsion will give a more opaque, chalky version of your colour as well as making it go further. If using the foam pad soak in water and squeeze out all excess water (it should be barely moist), dab on to your colour, then stamp most of it off on kitchen paper. There should be enough colour left to come off with a certain amount of pressure.

The commonest mistake made by beginners is to use far too much paint on the brush or sponge; this leads to the blobs and smudges so dreaded by novices, until they discover that flaws that leap out at you at close quarters become insignificant, even invisible, from a distance, submerged in the overall effect, especially when furnishings and pictures are back in place.

Left: A small border in white marches up one pine leg. This, like other stencils used in this book, is from the Paintability range of pre-cut plastic stencils. This one, which is part of a set, is called The Anatolian Living Room, after the rugs which inspired the designs.

Position the stencil and fix in place with tabs of masking tape. Pat the colour through the cut-outs with the brush or foam pad. (Tear off smaller bits of foam for finicky details where you need to be very accurate.) You will have planned beforehand which bits of the design will use which colours. It is not disastrous if you make a mistake – simply go over it again with the correct colour. Serious mistakes (for example if your arm was jogged and the brush or sponge went astray) can be wiped off immediately by rubbing with a damp cloth.

Repeat with the other colours, rinsing the brush or foam pad out in water each time and making it as dry as possible. Acrylic colours are instant-drying so the piece will be ready to varnish immediately. Over bare wood, as here, a matt or silk varnish looks more appealing; full gloss tends to give pine or other pale wood a factory-finished look, too plastic to suit stencils such as these. How many coats you use depends on how much wear you expect the piece to get. A child's desk could get quite a lot of punishment, so two or three coats with some rubbing down in between would be in order. Finish by rubbing gently with fine grade wet and dry paper, used wet and in a round-and-round action so as to cover every inch of surface.

Sometimes stencils can look too stark, or too vivid, on a painted or natural wood background. The trick here is to tone the decoration in with its surround by using a thin wash of one of the stencil colours (here it might be the green) rubbed over the whole surface with a clean rag. The old Norwegian rosmaling painters used to do this to soften the contrast between their vivid decorations and the painted backgrounds. If using one of the stencilled colours does not seem right, use a wash of diluted raw umber acrylic colour instead, in the antiquing manner. This can be wiped over with a rag, and wiped off here and there for highlights.

STENCILLING – STEP BY STEP

I. PREPARATION

The desk in its original state, nice enough with its old pine, but a little bit déjà vu. Start by planning how and where you want to position the stencil patterns. The Anatolian set includes a choice of narrow borders, a wide border, and the striking motif used on the desk top. As with the whole Paintability range, the books that enclose stencils give lots of photographic suggestions for colours and arrangements.

II. FIXING STENCILS

Having worked out where the stencils will go, the next step is to secure them (not necessary with a very small stencil) with tabs of sellotape or masking tape, so that they can be stencilled through without moving about. A foam pad was used to stencil in this case, for speed. Test the pad with paint on it on a piece of paper first, to find how little paint you need to make a clear print.

III. STENCILLING IN COLOUR

The creamy colour chosen as the main shade for the central star motif, has been stencilled through and a second colour added over the cream, for contrast. When stencilling in a light colour over a darker one, as here, it is best to stencil a white base on first. This means the pale colour will not lose its luminosity.

IV. STENCILS COMPLETE

The finished three-colour stencil scheme looks simple but attractive. When using more than one colour with one stencil, you may find it easier to use a brush rather than foam, because this can be directed more precisely. But making the foam into a really small wedge will also do the trick. On most items stencilled decoration should be protected with varnish, gloss or matt according to the style of the piece and the decoration. It is usual to give folk style pieces a non-shiny finish.

Right: Another view of the side of our little desk showing how sparsely the stencils have been used, but also how effective a little pattern can look. No need to overload surfaces.

TROMPE L'OEIL

TROMPE L'OEIL TOPS A TABLE

Strictly speaking all *faux* finishes come under the heading of *trompe l'oeil*, intended as they are to cheat the eye. However, the sense in which the term is generally used refers to a highly specialized form of painted illusionism, executed with the utmost realism, in which anything from shadowy niches harbouring alabaster statues to a butterfly hovering over a table top is so painted as to give the beholder a momentary conviction that what he or she sees is for real. But of course the illusion can only be momentary, because the image is not three-dimensional, and the most brilliant painted fake gives itself away close to, or when touched. The surprise of the deception gives way to amused appreciation of the artistic skill involved, which is usually considerable, and of the wit that planned and laid so cunning a visual trap. The element of magic involved in all figurative representation is especially present in a good example of *trompe l'oeil*. Even a detail is a certain crowd pleaser, and a touch of malice, as in the lifelike rendering of a banknote apparently dropped on the floor, only improves the joke.

Trompe l'oeil is quite often used, more functionally, to create a symmetry where there isn't one (for example a painted alcove to pair up with a real one) and to disguise dull things like cupboard doors behind painted scenes which look more attractive, such as that favourite subject – shelves of books in old leather bindings. A genuine bookcase might incorporate a cupboard for television, music centre etc.; in order to 'lose' this visual interruption,

Left: A pair of trompe l'oeil *postcards add an amusing and unexpected touch of decoration to a very plain small wood table. The joke is made richer when the writing on the postcard hints at some scandalous liaison, or makes a personal allusion to the owner of the table. Leaving the table as bare wood seems to add to the effectiveness of the* trompe l'oeil *surprise.*

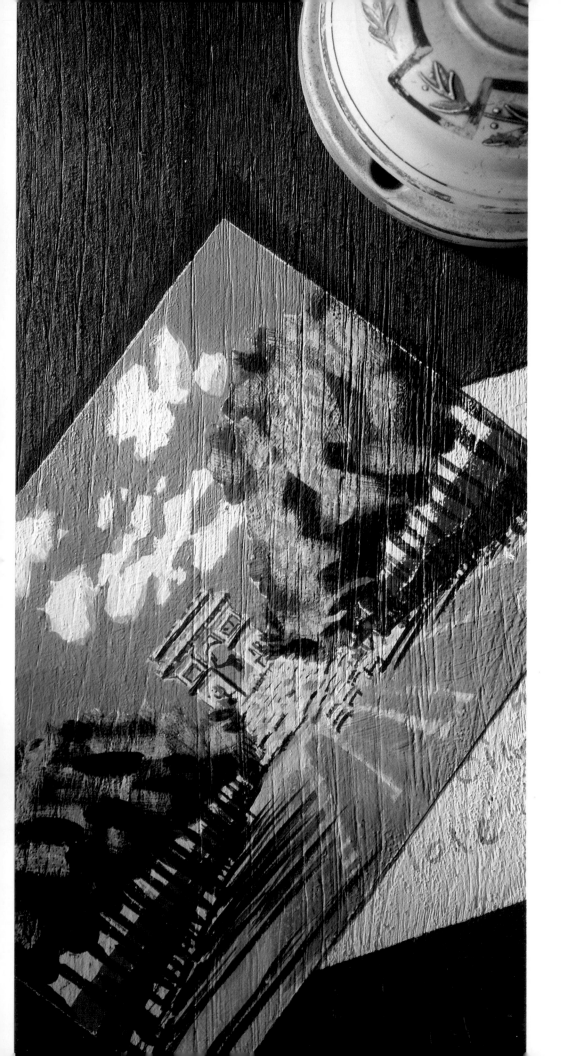

Left: You have to get this close to be undeceived. The wood grain showing through the paint is a give away. More layers of gesso could have made a perfectly smooth base.

TROMPE L'OEIL – STEP BY STEP

I. PREPARATION

The table was varnished, and quite shiny so as a preliminary the top was rubbed down with medium grade wire wool. Most trompe *painting is done on to a painted surface, sometimes given its own* faux *finish, like marble* pietra dura, *or graining. Playing cards are a favourite subject, partly because they look attractive and unmistakable, and partly because they are easy to copy.*

II. MASKING OFF

After some experiments, laying the postcards this way and that, this arrangement has been fixed on and the cards pencilled round on to the table. Masking tape was then stuck down round the pencil line, and the space inside filled in with white acrylic primer, giving several coats for a smooth, opaque white finish. The primer when dry can be rubbed down lightly with fine grade sandpaper for extra smoothness, since the idea is to imitate card.

III. CAREFUL COPYING

Using the cards as a reference, the picture and writing are copied as closely as possible on to the white base. It may be easier to pencil outlines in first. Here the scene was painted directly with the brush and artists' acrylic tube colours. The writing on the bottom card was done with a Rotring drawing pen. A real stamp is a cheeky touch.

IV. STAMPED, ADDRESSED AND VARNISHED

The final trick which gives trompe *painting a three dimensional quality is the painting in of realistic shadows. These can be exaggerated a little, for greater effect. If a series of objects are represented, it should be assumed that there is only one light source, so that all the shadows relate to it. Taking a photo (see page 154) of the* trompe *subjects in a mock-up, can be a great help to the sort of realism necessary for* trompe *painting.*

SPONGING

A SPARKLING SPONGE-DOWN

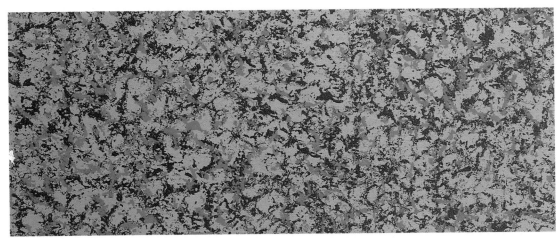

Anyone who is looking for a painless introduction to decorative finishes should try sponging, which is probably the easiest transformation of them all yet can give surprisingly sophisticated effects such as marble, granite, or the purely fantasy effect shown here vamping up a very plain but useful piece of furniture. In its original cream paint this small whitewood cabinet looks like bathroom furniture, something one would expect to pick up cheaply in a junkyard. Dressed up with sponging it looks good enough to be promoted to the living room.

All-over sponging like this, using a natural sponge to print an evenly distributed pattern, is especially suited to simple, functional shapes that need a bit of surface interest but nothing too dramatic or pretentious. It would be a good choice, for instance, for cheering up a run of kitchen units or a built-in bathroom suite you have inherited or got tired of. Sponged colour will give them a rich texture, a bit reminiscent of marbled paper, without making them stand out too much. You can choose much quieter colours than ours, of course, perhaps based on existing shades in the room, but a point to bear in mind is that even quite bright and contrasting colours like our scarlet, green and gold on pale blue are neutralized by being sponged on together in a balanced way, so that no colour predominates. The finished effect 'reads' as blue-green, but with a sparkle about it that comes from the red as well as the gold. The principle of balancing small areas of bright colour is of course demonstrated in many fabric patterns, as well as in

Left: A sponged piece has a knack of fitting in with its surroundings when the sponging colours, as here, pick up colours in the room. This sponging also has bright red mixed in with the blue and gold, but it is hardly noticeable from a distance.

traditional designs seen in, for example, Fair Isle knitting and Oriental rugs.

Studying any of these, and working out what colours have been combined for an effect you like, is an excellent way of coming up with a sponged colour combination you know will work. If the pattern is already part of the room – a curtain fabric perhaps, or a rug – you can work out a sponged colour scheme which will link up for a satisfyingly integrated effect.

A quite different sponged effect, more purely decorative, is arriving at by dabbing colour on apparently randomly, leaving more background colour showing, and massing the 'prints' to create patterns which can be sparse like animal footprints or as busy as a shower of confetti. This type of sponging has been used for centuries to decorate pottery quickly, and 'spongeware' crockery (now fashionable again) is useful for studying the effect. Usually you will find the sponging executed in two or more shades of one colour on a white ground. This always looks fresh and pretty, and would be a good effect for bedroom or nursery furniture. This type of sponging has a folksy charm, and is best suited to pieces with a rustic air – what is now being called 'country' furniture; it is also an ideal treatment for some of that not-so-appealing stripped pine. I would choose warmer colour mixes for non-bedroomy items such as dressers and blanket boxes; dark green on ochre with a detail or two picked out in dull red is an old Pennsylvania Dutch scheme, while reds and browns sponged on buff or red on black somewhat like crude tortoiseshell also turn up on antique pieces. Sponging on transparent colour, as in a transparent oil glaze, or an artists' acrylic tube colour mixed with acrylic medium (a transparent extender) will give a softer version of a sponged finish, nice for bathroom units and furniture or nursery pieces.

Above: The vitality of a sponged finish shows up well in this close-up of the cabinet. The random prints are all done for you when you use a natural sponge. Sponging is so easy the problem is knowing when to stop.

MATERIALS

1 litre matt emulsion base in pale blue; orange shellac; gold powder; methylated spirit; matchpot sizes (200ml) of scarlet and blue-green; sea sponge (go for a size that fits your hand and has plenty of holes for texture); saucers for holding different colours; standard brush for applying base coat; newspaper for testing 'prints'; clear matt, semi-gloss or gloss polyurethene varnish and varnish brush; fine grade wire wool.

METHOD

Give the piece two coats of base colour, thick enough to look even and opaque. Bare wood may need a first coat of primer, smoothly applied and lightly rubbed down for a smooth finish. Tip one of your sponge colours into a saucer. Dab the sponge into the paint and work off excess on waste paper. The prints should be crisp, not sloppy; this is arrived at by not overloading the sponge with paint, and by dabbing it on the surfaces firmly but lightly. A moment's practice on paper will show you how to arrive at the desired effect. Shift the sponge round from time to time to vary the texture of sponging. Emulsion hardens as it dries so rinse out the sponge occasionally, squeezing hard before you use it again to get as much water out as possible.

Sponge red quite evenly over all facets of the piece, leaving a good deal of base colour showing. By the time you have completed the first sponging colour, the piece should be dry, and you can go straight on to the second. Repeat with blue-green, filling in the blank spaces, but also overlapping here and there with the red. Mix the shellac with the gold powder to make an instant-drying gold paint, wash out the sponge and dry it before using it. Sponge lightly, as an 'accent', then wash the sponge clean in methylated spirit.

Stand back and look at the overall effect. Sponging is so easy and quick there is a danger of overdoing it, but this isn't a cause for anxiety – there is a simple way of evening out colours that have got too dense or blotchy. Just go over the piece again with the sponge and base colour to smooth out the finish visually.

Try to plan the sponging sequence so that you can work without smudging new colour – on the cabinet, for instance, sponge the back of the compartments first, then the sides, top and bottom. Sponging into corners is easier if you tear off a small piece of sponge just for this purpose.

On some sponged pieces you may want to pick out details such as knobs or mouldings with one of the sponging colours. A thin stripe of colour round tops, drawers etc. also looks smart and emphasizes good features and proportions. Do this when the sponging is dry, using the masking tape method described on page 43. Make sure the tape does not lift sponging paint off when you remove it. If this happens, varnish first, then do the striping.

The usefulness of varnish, as an isolating and protective coat between stages of a paint finish, is worth insisting upon because it is immensely encouraging when you are not quite sure how something will look to know that you can wipe it off and start again without damaging or disturbing the paint finish underneath. Professional painters use shellac for this purpose because it dries so quickly the work is hardly held up and also because the bleached type – otherwise known as White Polish – is as colourless as water. Remember to give a final coat of a tougher polyurethane varnish over the whole lot as protection.

Finish a sponged piece with one protective coat of matt, semi-gloss or gloss varnish, or two coats if it will be getting a lot of wear. Smooth the varnish with wire wool.

SPONGING – STEP BY STEP

I. PREPARATION

The first step as usual is to prepare the surface to take the base colour for the sponging, in this case a pale blue-grey matt emulsion. The cabinet had been painted before, and the paint was in a good state of repair, so all the preparation needed was to rub over the whole piece with medium grade sandpaper, paying special attention to the leading edges, or front edges, of the shelves and uprights.

II. BASE PAINTING

The cabinet has been given two coats of matt emulsion in the pale blue-grey chosen as the base colour. Key the base coat to colours in the room when working out a sponged colour combination. Then choose one deeper shade of the base coat, as here, one total contrast like our bright red, and perhaps substitute white for our gold. This would give a satisfactory formula for most rooms, especially where the sponging is required to merge with the background.

III. SPONGING COLOURS

Vivid red matt emulsion has been dabbed lightly over the entire piece using a small natural sponge which fits neatly into the palm of the hand. A large sponge covers the ground quicker but is harder to control. To sponge into awkward corners tear off a little piece of sponge and dab the colour in lightly. Practise sponge prints on a sheet of paper before launching off. Turn the sponge round now and then for variety. Wash out from time to time too.

IV. FINISHING

A second sponged coat, this time in a strong blue-green harmonizing with the base coat, covers in most, but not all the base left showing by the red sponging. Without making the piece look dark, the blue successfully 'knocks back' the brightness of the red prints and is on the way to creating a pointilliste colour harmony where lively contrasting dots of colour read, at a few steps distance, as a subtle tint with a changeable quality, like light itself. A quick sparkle of gold paint went over this, and then it was varnished.

Right: Red, blue and gold sponging looks crisp and characterful in a room full of faded greens and blues.

WOODWASH

WICKERWORK AWASH WITH COLOUR

I coined the term 'woodwash' for a currently top favourite finish on wood and wickerwork furniture which has the clear chalky colour of fresco painting on lime plaster or the transparency of watercolour washed over a white ground. The charm of woodwash lies in its luminous colour and the gentle variation of surface tone which adds greatly to the appeal of textures such as cane or wickerwork. We chose simple traditional objects – a set of old shopping baskets of sturdy shape and construction – to dramatize the radiance of the woodwash effect. The instructions given below are for creating your own woodwash colours over acrylic primer or gesso. Alternatively, House Style supplies ½ litre pots of woodwash in chalky pastels as well as more traditional country colours. This combines base with colour, so cutting out one process. Woodwash will adhere to any surface – wood, wicker, metal, even plastic – but shiny surfaces, whether varnished or inherently shiny like plastic, need rubbing down all over with fine wet-and-dry paper to roughen them and provide a key for the paint.

The DIY woodwash has the advantage in point of transparency of colour, and is best left unadorned. A feature of the House Style mix, however, is that by gentle, progressive sanding or rubbing with wire wool a very fine, almost porcelain texture and colour are achieved, which make an excellent background to stencils, penwork, or freehand painting. For a more complex effect one colour can be lightly dry-brushed over another.

Left: Luminous woodwash colour makes the most of the handsome ribbed wickerwork in a trio of old shopping baskets. The colour has been washed over a gesso base, and then dry-brushed lightly with white to create highlights.

113

Left: The chalky colours of some of the House Style Woodwash paints make a clutch of wooden balls in their blue basket look as fresh and springlike as sugared almonds.

WOODWASH – STEP BY STEP

I. PREPARATION

The basket au naturel, *its wicker given a thorough scrub in hot soapy water to remove old grime and grease. Some wicker items have been varnished. You can tell this by the shiny surface. The simplest way to deal with this is to rub it down quite hard with medium grade wire wool. This will break down the surface shine and provide a suitable surface for paint, primer or gesso. But go over the piece with a soft brush, or the suction hose of a vacuum cleaner, to remove tiny wire particles.*

II. PRIMING

Two coats of acrylic gesso, or acrylic primer (which is cheaper) are brushed over the basket, and worked well into the weave. The white base for woodwashing needs to be opaque for the transparent colour to register well. House Style Woodwash needs only one coat of primer, because its colour is opaque unless thinned with water. All these paints dry quickly, in minutes. A hairdryer can be used to speed things up even more if you are in a tearing hurry.

III. COLOUR-WASHING

A vivid blue wash of acrylic colour has been brushed over the white base, which soaks up the colour like blotting paper. This can also be done with a foam pad. Chalky pastels like our sugar almond colours work best with this technique; Mediterranean pinks, yellows, orange, aqua. For a range of darker colours suitable for folk type decoration, consult the House Style range, which includes navy, barn red and olive.

IV. DISTRESSING FOR HIGHLIGHTS

The final step in woodwashing is to create a bit more texture by dry-brushing highlights over the surface with white. Dry-brushing is a term that explains itself; just enough colour is left on the bristles to lay a very thin 'dry' brushstroke, usually needing some pressure. Rubbing back the woodwash to reveal some of the wicker colour beneath is another trick for enriching the surface. This can be combined with the dry-brushing. Alternatively try brushing colour over colour for a different sort of richness.

SPATTERING

A RASH OF COLOUR

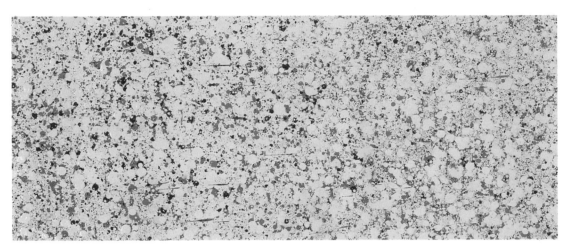

Spattering creates an effect somewhat similar to sponging but more controlled and precise in appearance, with showers of tiny dots of colour creating an intriguing speckled effect, rather like a bird's egg. There is a knack to spattering, so that the spatters are neat and round and distributed fairly evenly. This makes it appear more difficult than sponging, for instance, but in practice it only takes a short practice run on a sheet of paper to develop control and accuracy. After that the process goes with a swing and can be used to enliven quite large areas of paintwork very rapidly. Another point in its favour, in some people's eyes, is that you can spatter without getting paint on your hands.

On the other hand, the spattered colour tends to cover a fairly wide area around the piece you are working on, unless you come in very close, which is apt to create less even spotting. One solution of course is to work outside, on a fine day. Another is to fix up a painting corner by sellotaping sheets of newspaper or plastic dust sheets to both walls, laying a few more on the floor. Professional painters work on jobs like these in a plastic tent but their spray guns create a great deal more 'fall out' than a brush jogged on a stick. Stand your piece in the corner, and you should have no problems from straying paint spots. With a piece like our chair, it may also be helpful to fix up a temporary stand (an old trunk, or a table with a plastic sheet over it) to let you get at the legs easily without having to kneel on the floor. The piece will have to be turned round so you can deal with each surface separately.

Left: The simple spatter colour scheme of dark blue and dark red over pale cream used to brighten up a plain wooden chair pick up colours used in this painted bathroom setting. It is surprising how a light sprinkling of well-chosen colour 'dresses' a piece of furniture and ties it in to its setting.

Spattered colour usually dries on contact so the piece can be handled safely. Invariably your first attempt will look uneven, with patches where one colour has registered more strongly than the other. This can look attractive, and folksy, but if you are determined on even, regular, spots the solution is simple – finish up by re-spattering the whole piece with the base colour.

Historically, spatter techniques seem to have been used at first to imitate naturally speckled substances, like granite and porphyry. There was a vogue for these *faux* finishes during the late 18th century, their subdued decorativeness marrying well with the strict shapes and ormolu trimmings characteristic of the Empire style. Sweden, a country where granite is common and the much rarer porphyry exists in a subtle range of colours, seems to have gravitated naturally towards the use of spattered effects in interior decoration and Swedish painters developed all sorts of variations on the theme, from discreet speckles to bold and splashy patterns of dots and dashes (the latter are drips, it must be acknowledged) flicked over surfaces with a small whisk of birch twigs. The boldest of these effects seem to have been worked up to give a wallpaper effect in the early 19th century, when Swedish wallpapers were all imported and very expensive. Their effectiveness demonstrates that spattering does not have to be technically controlled and perfect to be highly decorative, but can look splendidly lively executed with the freedom of action painting. These effects belong to a provincial and peasant tradition of great vigour, using the rich, friendly colours typical of old Scandinavian wooden cottages and furniture – brown-red, corn yellow, silver grey, flat green and a deep blackish blue. Grey, white and black spatters on brown-red are one popular formula, often used on dados, while white, black and brown-red on yellow is another striking example. Spattering is most effective on plain surfaces and simple shapes.

Both are much in evidence here in the rather big-boned wooden chair of undistinguished lines, to which spattering has given a whole new chic, reminiscent of the elegant packaging adopted by one of London's most exclusive suppliers of bathroom treats.

MATERIALS

1 litre matt emulsion in pale cream for base; matchpot sizes (200ml) of contrast matt emulsion in dark blue and dark red; standard decorators' paintbrush in 2½ inch/6cm size with bushy bristles; stick, ruler or wooden spoon handle to jog the saucers for mixing colour; newspapers, masking tapes and tacks for masking; clear semi-gloss or gloss polyurethane varnish and varnish brush; fine grade wire wool.

METHOD

Bare wood may need priming first. Then paint a base coat with cream emulsion to give a thick, shadowless surface. Thin your first spatter colour with a little water and stir to mix; the consistency should be more fluid than standard emulsion, but not watery. Start by adding 1 tablespoon of water to 200ml and test by spattering on paper from a distance of about 3 ft/90cm. To spatter, take up some colour on the brush, working it into the bristles. Shake over paper to remove the surplus, then, with the stick held in your left hand, (reverse the procedure if you are left-handed) tap the brush handle down briskly on to the stick to release a spray of dots. If the dots are clumsy the mixture may need more thinning; if they run, the mixture is too watery. Adjust, and repeat until you are getting a nice clear spatter effect.

Before spattering the piece, fix newspaper all around it with masking tape and tacks to catch spatter which goes wide. Spatter one facet at a time in the way described, keeping at

Left: Moving closer in one can see how distinctly the coloured dots register against the pale base, and how the dark blue prevails over the brighter red, keeping more or less to the given ratio of the two colours in the room. This is a fun finish to do, giving a very chic and professional effect.

approximately the same distance from the surface – between 2 and 3 ft/60 and 90cm. On a piece like our chair, with so many corners and angles, the spatter tends to build up on the leading edges which have received a double dose of colour. The remedy for this is to finish by spattering with the base colour to even things up again, so there is no need to worry about it. When the piece has been speckled lightly all over in one colour, go back over it with the other, aiming for even distribution of colours but leaving plenty of base showing (more than when you are sponging). Stand back for an overall view, then spatter the base

colour, thinned as before, over patchy areas to even them up. You might decide on a further spatter coat in a different colour; white always softens the effect, while black sharpens it up. Antique furniture painted in the normal way and then glazed was sometimes given a final fine spatter in a darker tone of the glaze colour or in black to subtly add age and texture to the paintwork, and this is a quick and effective finishing touch to remember. Spattering with metallic paint made by mixing gold or bronze powder and shellac adds a touch of sparkle which can be charming.

Spattered paint dries almost the instant it connects, so the spattered item can be varnished immediately. Varnish enhances spattered surfaces, bringing out the colours. A chair requires at least two coats of clear varnish because it gets so much wear and tear, but one may be enough on other pieces. Once the varnish is dry, go lightly over it with fine grade wire wool, to give a really silky feel to the surfaces. If you fancy the natty look of painted line trim, this is the time to do it, either freehand (slips of the hand can be wiped clean over varnish) or with masking tape. The trim will need a final coat of varnish.

SPATTERING – STEP BY STEP

I. PREPARATION

The chair was already painted, with old gloss paint, so this was rubbed back with coarse and medium grade sandpapers to smooth it down and provide a good 'key' for subsequent paint coats. Pay special attention when rubbing down to edges, corners, and inner angles, folding paper into little 'blades' to cut into tricky places. Paint tends to build up in all these spots. If you then add more paint coats on top, the result is a blurring of the crisp lines of the piece, in this case the chief attraction of the chair.

II. BASE PAINTING

A smooth, opaque base for spattering has been given to the chair with two coats of creamy matt emulsion, brushed on evenly and very lightly smoothed over with fine grade wire wool after the second coat has dried. Always take special care when rubbing back emulsion paints, because you only want to smooth off hairs, dust, nibs etc, not to puncture or break the 'skin' formed by this type of paint.

III. SPATTERED COLOURS

Using a standard paint brush, jogged on a stick, the first spatter coat of dark blue has been applied over most of the chair. Spattering inaccessible bits like the inside legs takes patience and a lot of adjusting, by turning the chair upside down, standing it on a box, and so on. You will find that by coming in close, with a bit of practice, you can direct the spray of colour quite accurately. Some painters claim that spattering at an angle to the piece helps control the colour. It is never time wasted to rehearse for a few minutes first.

IV. FINISHING

A red spatter coat has gone over the blue, rather lighter in density of spots. Note the spatter colour which has strayed on to the newspaper backing. Because watery spatter colour dries almost instantly you can proceed at once to the final process, which gives a professional-looking lightness and evenness to the piece. This consists simply of spattering over the red and blue with the creamy base colour, paying special attention to patches where colour has built up unevenly. It is almost impossible, for instance, to avoid a build-up of colour along leading edges. Finish by varnishing.

Right: Colour breaks out all over in this paint rash close-up. Not all the spatters are perfectly round and even, but a final sprinkle of base colour evens things out miraculously.

MASTERCLASS

It is by doing rather than reading about it that one progresses from the tentative dabs of the beginner to the experienced painter's fluent and confident brushwork. However there has to be an incentive to keep initial enthusiasm going and what could be more inspiring than the following series of

Masterclasses where professional decorative painters talk about their favourite pieces and give an interesting and detailed account of how they arrived at their own specialized effects, from the very first ideas of design to the flourish and shine of the final coat of varnish.

PENWORK
WRITING ON THE TABLE

Penwork is a type of pen-and-ink decoration that was popular in the late 18th and early 19th centuries for embellishing smaller items of furniture and bibelots. Its inspiration seems to have been the delicate and elaborate carved ivory that came from India. Penwork requires patience and taste rather than creative originality; its first enthusiasts seem to have been quite content to copy from contemporary prints. For young ladies taking drawing lessons, penwork must have seemed a suitable exercise for practice in copying from an original, building up a design, shading and so forth. The results were charming and sometimes spectacular, as with the large writing desk entirely covered with filigree penwork in the furniture collection of the Victoria and Albert Museum in London.

The attraction of penwork is that dashingly decorative flourishes can be added to furniture and small items from picture frames to tea caddies with the simplest equipment. Now that photocopiers are so accessible there is no need to buy original prints – suitable motifs and vignettes can be photocopied from books and magazines to build up a collection of black and white images. Practise on a little wooden box, tray or frame to build up confidence. (See page 82).

As our table shows there is no need to cover an entire surface, though on a small object you may prefer to. Be warned; penwork is slow, and cannot be rushed, but it makes a pleasant ongoing activity. The sort of furniture that penwork sets off admirably is that of stylish, simple shape, in pine rather than hardwood, attractive rather than valuable. It can also be used to add interest to reproduction pieces. The background to decorative work can be plain black, wood grained as shown, painted, or simply stained and varnished. Look at old examples for ideas.

Your work will go faster and more easily if the surface you are decorating can be laid flat. Almost certainly old pieces were inked before being made up, and this is the ideal. Take doors off hinges and work at them on a table;

Left: A relatively small area of penwork gives a great deal of interest and glamour to what started out as a shapely but humble deal washstand. The combination of sharp decoration in black and white with rich rosewood graining is typical of Regency furniture.

drawer fronts are easy enough to balance on one's knees and little items present no problems. However, with larger items you will have to resign yourself to moving the piece around so that each surface can be tackled in turn.

My table was picked up cheaply years ago in a junk shop; I liked its lyre-shaped legs and curvaceous base. It was topless so I had a slab of washstand marble cut to fit (it was made as a washstand originally, so marble seemed appropriate). The wood is pine. I began by stripping it but it looked disappointingly ordinary. The rosewood graining and penwork treatment came to me after admiring a stylish Regency cabinet at an antiques fair. Rosewood graining is one of the most effective *faux* finishes, much used during the Regency period.

MATERIALS

For graining Satin finish oil-based paint in a light red shade, softened if necessary with burnt umber oil colour. The glaze for graining consisted of black and burnt umber oil colours mixed with a little proprietary transparent oil glaze, thinned with white spirit to a watery consistency. A long-bristled flogger brush is a justifiable expense if you plan to do much graining – the bristles are designed to be flexible and responsive, clumping naturally to give the bold striping typical of rosewood graining.

For penwork decoration Acrylic primer; fine grade wire wool; fine grade wet-and-dry paper; dip pen-nibs in various widths plus a holder; a fine brush such as Winsor and Newton Sceptre 101 range sizes 1 and 3; Indian ink; Tipp-Ex erasing fluid; shellac; clear gloss polyurethane varnish; standard brush to apply acrylic primer; varnish brush for shellac; methylated spirit; carbon paper; pencil; containers for mixing glaze etc.; soft rags or kitchen paper; ruler.

GRAINING METHOD

The table was already painted, with blackboard paint. I gave it two coats of red paint, rubbing down with wet-and-dry paper dipped into water to smooth it before graining – the smoother the surface, the easier it is to draw on.

Above: The same penwork panel arrangement, of twining classical flora enclosed in a border of pearls, decorates each of the four sides of the table top. Pearls were a favourite element in 18th-century decoration, edging chair backs, box tops, table tops. Adam's suite for the Osterley Etruscan Room is heavily pearled. Note other examples of penwork and penwork type subjects on the table. The metal box combines printed black and white borders glued in place, with penwork detail while the printed frame features just the sort of small classical motif which translates well into black and white decoration.

The rosewood graining was done one surface at a time – first the legs, then the top, and finally the base. To achieve bold but not rigidly straight markings, brush a coat of glaze over the surface in question, thinly and evenly. With the flogger brush go over the wet glaze rapidly, 'dragging' it to form irregular stripes. These should follow the direction real wood grain would take on an item of furniture. A slight wrist wobble here and there introduces a ripple into the grain markings. Some of the red base should be left showing.

Where horizontal graining butts up against vertical, as at the ends of the table top, use strips of masking tape to block off the horizontally grained section. Grain as described, allow to dry then peel off the tape and drag the brush vertically over the remaining space. Care over details like these is of more importance than a thorough knowledge of rosewood markings.

PENWORK DECORATION METHOD

When the graining was dry I used acrylic primer to paint in the white areas to be decorated with penwork. The white ground needs to be thick, even and smooth, like paper. Two or three coats, rubbed down when dry (acrylic primer dries in minutes) gave the right surface. I brushed over this with shellac, also fast drying, and rubbed it down lightly once dry. Shellac gives a mellow, ivory tinge to the white as well as a sleek surface for the pen.

I used carbon paper to trace off my design on to the white areas. Coloured chalk can be used to touch up the traced outlines – it is easier to wipe off than pencil. It is unnerving to start right in with the pen and ink, but comfort yourself that Tipp-Ex makes corrections a lot easier than they were in the 18th century. Rehearse the main shapes a few times on paper with your various nibs to gain fluency; you will get smoother and more accomplished effects quite quickly, especially if you are doing repeat patterns like those shown.

Everyone who tries penwork will discover his or her favourite method of proceeding; this is mine. First I outline the shapes and add the main internal lines, such as central veins on leaves.

Next, with the brush, I fill in the background with ink. Lastly I go over each bit of the pattern, shading in with very fine lines and tidying up the outlines. After the fine detail has been done I find it helps to move on to a second section so that I can come back to the first with a fresh eye later and decide if the shading needs strengthening. Any mistakes can be blotted out easily with Tipp-Ex; it dries in seconds and can be gone over again immediately with ink. An extra dab of shellac on top will soften the whiteness down to match the rest. I decided to add a border of 'pearls' after completing the inset panel, and I found Tipp-Ex made a more opaque base, added in blobs, than the acrylic primer.

When the penwork is complete, and has had 24 hours to dry hard, go over it all with cottonwool dipped in warm water and wrung out to clean off your chalk or pencil marks. Do not rub too hard to begin with; Indian ink is waterproof but sometimes fingermarks make it adhere less well.

PROTECTIVE FINISHES

You will certainly want to give your handsome decoration a protective finish to guard it against handling and knocks. I used two coats of standard shellac over the penworked areas to mellow the colour to ivory rather than white, as well as to protect the decoration. I rubbed this down very gently with fine wire wool and then gave the whole table two coats of clear gloss polyurethane varnish, allowing plenty of drying time in between and finishing up with a final smoothing session with the fine wet-and-dry paper, used damp, to cut the shine a little and give a silky texture. Some professionals prefer to end up with a coat of clear semi-gloss polyurethane varnish, on top of the gloss varnish, because this gives depth to the finish without being too shiny. A lot will depend on how much use you expect your piece to get; a masterpiece which was months in the making deserves the most thorough protection you can give it and varnishing is, I find, a deeply satisfying task in itself. In any event, remember that this is the sort of decorative item that becomes a family heirloom, so take pains over the final varnishing.

DRY PAINT VARNISHES

IN THE FOOTSTEPS OF DUNCAN AND VANESSA

Art students used to be sent to make copies of famous paintings because the act of copying teaches more about a painter's style than a series of lectures. In a rather similar way, the witty and accomplished style-of-Omega-Workshop painted furniture produced by a young Sussex College of Art graduate, Robert Campling, and shown at Charleston, the home of Omega's founder members, Vanessa Bell and Duncan Grant, provides fascinating insights into what is, and what is not, typical of their highly individual decorative style.

'Typically Omega' would seem to mean using a 'dry' paint texture, a muted palette of chalky colours, conspicuous brushwork and a primitivist style influenced by the French Post-Impressionists. Robert Campling is not consciously thinking any of this as he works on one of his Omega pastiches, such as the table in our picture; it is more that having steeped himself in the Omega group's style and colours, he almost can't help doing things their way and arriving at remarkably similar results.

It all began when Robert was getting together his final art school project as a textile student. His textile designs were based on work by the Omega group, and he had the idea of painting furniture in the same style to go with the fabrics. One result of this was an invitation to show the painted furniture at Charleston to help with the Charleston Trust's fund-raising efforts, and this has led to so many private commissions to decorate rooms and furniture that he now seems to be moving out of textile design in favour of decorative painting.

Robert thinks the individual use of colour is the most typical characteristic. 'The Omega artists mainly used rather dusty colours, but with vivid bits of lemon yellow or bright blue, and lots of dark colours for contrast, so the whole effect is quite bright really. I found the effect went down better with American visitors to Charleston. Though the Brits liked it they thought

Left: The casual confidence of a design and colour scheme inspired by the Omega style makes a completely different piece from the quaint, rather than beautiful, workbox-cum-table in fumed oak shown here. Though certainly not Duncan or Vanessa's style of piece it does belong to their period, 1920s going on 1930s.

they might not be able to live with it, but the Americans just went for it.'

The table, like most of the pieces shown at Charleston (and now mostly sold) was a 'piece of junk' picked up for next to nothing in one of the Brighton car boot sales which Robert used to patronise as an impecunious art student.

'The lid lifts up, and there's a sort of box underneath,' he says. 'I suppose it's a Twenties or Thirties piece. It had a horrible varnished veneered finish when I got it.'

He stripped this back using acetone, which he finds an effective solvent for all sorts of old finishes. It has to be applied in the open air, and Robert wears plastic gloves and an industrial-type mask, which hardware stores and some chemists can supply.

MATERIALS

Liquitex acrylic gesso; artists' oil tube colours in a range of colours – burnt sienna, indigo, ochre, black, white, vermilion, alizarin crimson, lemon yellow, cobalt, burnt umber; hogshair fitches in varying sizes; white spirit; Craig and Rose Extra Pale Dead Flat Varnish and varnish brush.

METHOD

Having stripped off the original varnish to reveal bare wood, Robert gave the whole piece two coats of acrylic gesso as a primer. He applied it unthinned, and quite thickly and brushily for a deliberately rough and textured look, which is an Omega trademark. It is noticeable that Robert's list of materials omits sandpaper, wire wool, or other abrasives used to create smooth, sleek paint surfaces. However, on the table top, which will be handled and wiped, the gesso base is laid on quite smoothly, without pronounced brushmarks.

He then painted the table using artists' oil tube colours thinned with white spirit and applied directly over the acrylic gesso base. If the colours are well thinned, this creates the 'dry' texture so characteristic of the pieces painted by Vanessa Bell and Duncan Grant. The gesso blots up the oiliness. The Omega style of casual brushwork grows out of a technique using colour thinly, in a painterly way, rather than building up layers of it in various media as a craftsman does.

This approach does not allow much correction or overpainting – in fact, mistakes have to be painted out with more acrylic gesso. Robert starts on a piece with a 'very rough' idea of what he wants to do with it in terms of colours, design and general feel. Sometimes he makes sketches beforehand, on paper which can help to clarify a picture in his mind's eye when he begins using the brush. Usually he will start brushing in the straightforward bits, in this case the table legs and stretchers, and the plain framework to the decorative panels on the 'box'. These are brushed over with a drab olive green in a casual sketchbook fashion, not to cover, but to dramatize. Dabs of black on the leg joints are equally casual. This is not a style for the perfectionist type, who likes neatness and symmetry; it is a splash and scribble approach, yet it needs to be done with conviction or it looks a mess. Its effect on furniture is intriguing, because it obliterates it as furniture of a particular period style. Whatever you start with, pine dresser or fumed oak bedhead, what you end up with is a piece of Omega, vivacious, expressive and immensely decorative. Craft-based critics who mark down Omega group's furniture on the grounds that it was carelessly painted and amateurish seem to miss the point, which is that primitivism – a sort of inspired slapdashness – is the aim.

Left: This close-up shows how loosely impressionistic the brushwork on the table is, and how a very simple motif like the candle can build up with repetition into an arresting and decorative border. Notice the use of black, essential to beef up Omega style pastels.

But the top is the eyecatcher, a sprightly bullseye of concentric rings of pattern and colour, each one of which looks casually added, on the spur of the moment, but which all add up to a thoroughly sophisticated and satisfactory looking table top, on which a primitivistic genuine Omega lamp and shade look quite at home. The table was photographed in Clive Bell's room at Charleston, which has quite a bit of decorative painting on walls and furniture (sections appear at both sides of the main picture) so Campling's skill at pastiche was put to a fairly searching test. Patterns on the table top – loops, dots of bright colour – are typical of the way Duncan Grant covered surfaces with decorative doodles, scribbling round a fireplace or looping round a ceramic plate. The effect has a freshness which is charming. The ring of candles pointing inwards, which makes a strong border to the table top, was a theme in the exhibition dreamed up by Robert. 'Candles and lots of dark colours', he says cryptically.

Robert worked out the theme of the panels in his head before starting on them. Each panel shows an oval dressing table-type mirror on a stand, and in the mirror a different reflection – a pot of geraniums, a vase of poppies, the painter's own profile. There is a lot of lively brushwork, the mirror has saffron squiggles on its frame which nicely pick up saffron loops on the table top; the colours are warm, with lots of dusty fleshy pink and nutty browns, with bits of red, blue and green for contrast, creating a soft but rich effect.

Finally, after being left to dry for several days (less would do) the table was given two coats of Craig and Rose Extra Pale Dead Flat Varnish. This is the only possible type of varnish to use with this style of decoration – anything even faintly reflective or shiny would destroy the 'dry' surface which is so much the basis of its appeal to the eye.

FINE ART

THE GOTHIC SCREEN

Neither Marianna Kennedy nor Jim Howett, two young designers operating out of Spitalfields in London's East End, would describe themselves as decorative painters; Jim designs and makes furniture, Marianna paints pictures. But sometimes they get together on interesting projects like the strange and handsome Gothic screen, one of a series of screens they produced until the idea ran out of steam, as creative ideas are apt to do. Their joint work is always arresting, as one would expect from two powerful imaginations working together. Both from North America (Marianna a Canadian of Irish extraction, Jim a mid-Westerner), they both combine a liking for the bizarre and surreal with a strong practical streak, and their work fairly jumps with originality.

Usually Jim designs and makes the furniture and Marianna paints and decorates it. In the case of the Gothic screen the division was less tidy; Jim made the three-panel screen from hand-planed pine for Marianna to decorate, but he also worked on the gilded Gothic tracery. A bookbinder friend, Charles Gledhill, came up with the idea of impressing gold stars on the dark sky with a bookbinder's tool, which he showed them how to use. There is an improvisatory spirit about the way this team works which can come up with exciting results, and this is particularly evident in their easy attitude to technique.

'We aren't so interested in technique,' Marianna says, meaning that their work is led by ideas, rather than by craftsmanship for its own sake. However, if a technique is called for, including demanding ones such as oil gilding and *craquelure*, Marianna can be relied upon to work on it and get it right. She served an apprenticeship of sorts in oil gilding (in which transfer leaf is applied over oil-based gold size), working with a team of 20 men re-gilding the main ceiling of the RAC club in London's St James. The experience of working with oil-based size helped her to master the sensitive, almost intuitive timing which is the secret of successful *craquelure*. She has

Left: Screens look wonderful filling a corner, or backing a fireside chair. The Howett/Kennedy joint effort shown here has a mysterious medieval quality enhanced by gilding and craquelure varnish.

135

look massively and mysteriously aged. The French *craquelure* system she employs is based on using water and oil-based varnish; the different drying speed produces the cracks.

MATERIALS

Traditional gesso, made from whiting and rabbit-skin glue; fine and medium grade sandpaper; Plaka casein-based paints – white was used to base-coat the decorative panels, red was the base for the gilding, simulating the reddish tone of traditional red bole, the gilder's ground for gold leaf (other Plaka colours were used, in small quantities, for decoration); three-hour oil-based size; six books of Dutch Metal transfer leaf, like a bright gold but cheaper; Lefranc et Bourgeois *craquelure*; pen and Indian ink; raw and burnt umber artists' oil tube colour; white spirit; assorted brushes, from fine sables to hogshair fitches, plus an old brush for applying gesso.

METHOD

Marianna used traditional gesso made with whiting and warmed rabbit-skin glue, or size, mixed together to a smooth cream and applied warm to the wood. She brushed it out

also spent some time in Italy working on commission from Milanese clients and she has a theory that the Italian climate makes working with problematic ingredients, like gold size, much easier. 'Here the climate is so much more damp it can take eight hours for a three-hour size to go off,' she explains. 'You have to experiment many times to get it right.'

Her *craquelure* was perfected in New York, crackling varnish over a French handblocked paper in 145 colours to make it thinly, left it to dry, then re-coated it. In all she applied eight coats of soft size followed by hard size in the Italian fashion. Hard size has more glue, soft size more whiting, and the alternation makes for the toughest and best-bonded underlay for paint. Each coat was sanded smooth before applying the next. (Traditional gesso is a material worth mastering for a professional, serious decorative painter. The amateur just having fun, or looking to provide a more than usually flawless base for painting, would be best advised to use the commonly available acrylic gesso, which is fast-drying and as simple to apply as paint.)

The images for the painted panels are a development of a series of small paintings on wood which Marianna completed a year or so ago. Their subject matter combines elements of Renaissance drawings, worked into a kind of narrative. One panel shows a Tuscan landscape, another a castello on top of a steep hill, the third, and most disturbing, the 'fiery mountain' – red flames licking out of a conical hill.

'I honestly didn't think it out, I just went ahead and painted it intuitively, to look rather mysterious,' she explains.

She drew the subjects out in pencil, by eye, not measuring. Then she painted them using Plaka paints.

'Plaka is a fantastic paint, I find,' she says. 'It is fast-drying and water-based, but it responds well to glazes and it burnishes up nicely.' By this she means that a Plaka painted surface can be rubbed back with fine grade sandpaper or wire wool more satisfactorily than the plasticized emulsion paints, giving a superior texture.

After completing the panels, Marianna and Jim drew out the Gothic framework, colouring it in red Plaka to simulate red bole. The rest was painted black.

After sizing over the red areas with three-hour size, Marianna kept a vigilant eye on its speed of drying. The trick is to catch the size when it is almost dry, but still just tacky enough to make a kind of snapping noise if you rap it with your knuckles. Dutch Metal transfer leaf, the sheets cut to fit with a little bit over, were overlapped a fraction as they were pressed down on to the size. Then the paper backing was very carefully peeled away. The gold leaf was left overnight, then smoothed down gently and carefully with a soft brush or silk cloth, the loose bits being removed. Jim drew details over the leaf with pen and Indian ink, as shown.

Both the gilding and the painted panels were treated next with the *craquelure* finish using the two separate varnishes, one oil-, one water-based, which are supplied with the kit. After a fine crackle or crazing had developed satisfactorily, Marianna rubbed thinned umber oil tube colour over the crackle to darken it and give an instant air of antiquity. The raw dazzle of the Dutch Metal is also considerably softened and mellowed by this ageing rub over, and the whole tonality of the piece comes together. This is one of the most satisfying stages of decorative painting on furniture, when all the somewhat tedious preliminaries are triumphantly justified.

Before the screen was quite complete, the dark night sky above the Gothic crockets needed its quota of gold. The bookmaking friend showed how the metal stamp used in stamping and gilding on leather bindings could be heated and then pressed down over a scrap of gold into the painted surface, leaving a crisp little gilt ornament sunk into a minute depression in the painted surface at the top of the screen. The same technique was used over the back of the screen, which needed to be made respectable enough to be shown, without getting the full decorative works.

WATER-BASED PAINTS
SCANDINAVIAN STYLE

Belinda Ballantyne is fast making a name for herself as both a practitioner and a teacher of decorative paint techniques. She runs regular courses in the Wiltshire countryside, as well as teaching and demonstrating at interior decorating schools in London. She is largely self-taught and has learned mainly by practice, which is usually the best way – given talent and determination to start with. Her painting style is flexible and innovative, as any professional's needs to be, but she is probably most at home working in the folk-classic idiom of the Italian/Scandinavian (her phrase) bureau shown here. Gentler colours, poised use of traditional motifs and, above all, a penchant for the delicate translucency of water-based paints give her work a rustic elegance which is very much in the spirit of the times.

Belinda's bureau is a piece she bought in a closing-down sale five years ago in London's Chelsea, having fallen for 'the curvy shape of the door panels and the appealing details, like all the little cubby holes inside'. It is important to her that a piece for painting has 'good bone structure', and this was what her bureau abundantly provided. 'However well you paint you can't change the basic shape of a piece,' she points out. She deliberately put the bureau aside until she felt ready to do it justice. 'I thought of it as the cherry on the cake – one day, when I'd learnt an awful lot more, I would paint it quite beautifully'.

The decision to give it a Scandinavian rococo treatment grew quite naturally from a recent trip to Norway where she went in search of new ideas, techniques and colours in traditional painted furniture and decoration. In fact, given that it is pine, and unusually well crafted, it is not impossible that the bureau originally came from Scandinavia, perhaps Sweden, and was painted like most softwood pieces. Belinda did not know this when she bought the piece but her trip to Norway convinced her that it was the right shape for a Scandinavian-style decorative treatment.

Left: A full length view of Belinda's Scandinavian styled bureau, taken in her studio, shows how ingeniously she has replicated the double-arch moulding on the doors in the painted scheme she devised for the drawers and desk lid.

139

'I so love their colour schemes,' she says, 'I had no difficulty deciding what colours to paint my bureau. Prussian blue, yellow ochre and English red it had to be.'

MATERIALS

Proprietary wax remover; Dulux matt emulsion in Softwater and Serenade for the base; acrylic artists' oil tube colour, with acrylic medium, for lining; standard artists' watercolours in pans in Prussian blue, red oxide and yellow ochre for decorative painting; large fitch; small varnish brush; sable watercolour brushes in sizes 9 and 12; coach liners in 1 inch/2.5 cm and 2½ inch/6.3 cm lengths; Wondersize; Dutch Metal transfer leaf; blackboard chalk; set of cookie cutters for templates; standard shellac; fine-grade wire wool; ruler; Craig and Rose Extra Pale Dead Flat Varnish; white spirit; methylated spirit for cleaning brushes, thinning varnish.

METHOD

All Belinda had clearly in mind when she began work on the bureau was the Norwegian-inspired colour scheme and the idea of using the double-arched shape of the fielded panels on the bureau doors to make painted panels on the drawers and desk flap. She had also decided to use water-based paints throughout.

The first step was to remove the existing waxed finish, using a proprietary wax remover which is simply wiped on and wiped off again. She repeated this until the wood 'felt not the slightest bit greasy to my fingertips'. Any wax left on would have interfered with the adhesion of the water-based emulsion paints. The handles and escutcheons were removed.

Belinda painted the whole bureau in pale blue emulsion, applying it directly over the wood, without undercoat or primer. 'I wanted the paint to have that slight touch of

Above: The 'worn away' effect, typical of Belinda's 'Scandinavian-style' shows up well.

transparency you see in the old Scandinavian painted pieces, with the wood grain just showing through.'

She brushed the blue over one facet at a time, brushing with the grain. When this dried she found it 'too new-looking' and went over the entire piece with standard shellac thinned down with methylated spirit. The orange tone of the shellac gave a greeny tinge to the blue, and a slightly streaky tone.

The next step was to rough out panels on the bottom part of the bureau, the desk flap and drawers, to match the panels on the top. Using cookie cutters and odd plates and saucers as templates, blackboard chalk (easier to rub off than pencil) and a ruler, she began by plotting out the larger panel on the desk flap. She made a chalk mark in the centre of the flap and set the panel 3¼ inches/8 cm from the top and 2¾ inches/7 cm from the bottom of the flap because this looked more satisfactory.

Each decorated drawer panel is slightly deeper than the one above it, but the ends are all aligned. Belinda arrived at the right shapes for the double-rounded ends by experimenting with her cookie cutters and odd crocks until the effect looked right and convincing.

When the shapes were chalked in she filled them in with matt off-white emulsion, using a large fitch and small varnish brush for neatening the edges, and going with the grain. The colour was a bit patchy when dry because of the blue underneath, but Belinda liked that too. To do the lining she used the 2½ inch/6.3 cm coachliner with cadmium red light acrylic colour mixed with a little acrylic medium to make it transparent and flow more easily. She did the lining freehand, using the smaller 1 inch/2.5 cm brush for the curved ends of the panels.

'It's easier with the coachliners because you can get to the end of a line without running out of colour,' she explains.

After studying photographs and sketches she brought back from Norway, she was ready to block in the 'squirlies' with blackboard chalk. These scrolling shapes are typical of Scandinavian rococo painted decoration.' Belinda wanted the transparency of watercolour for her scrolling. The red touches were her own idea. 'I tried out different combinations of shapes and colours on a sample board until I liked the effect,' she says.

She painted the larger 'squirlies' using large sable watercolour brushes and a fairly watery solution of Prussian blue. 'It needs to be watery enough to sink into the emulsion, but not so watery it runs.'

The scrolls needed shading to bring them to life. For this she fixed on an imaginary light source at top left, so all scrolls were lighter on the left, darker on the right side. She kept to the same limited palette for this, using ochre for lights, stronger blue tinged with red for the darks.

Belinda recommends starting on the least important facet because this tends to be less assured. She found her first panels on the drawers were a bit too strongly coloured, so she softened this effect on the desk flap and doors and then went over the too-bright 'squirlies' with a cotton bud and water to lift off some of the colour and soften them.

Gilding was often used to give sparkle and richness to the grander Scandinavian pieces. Belinda used Dutch Metal transfer leaf rather than pure gold leaf for speed and ease of application. Wondersize is an Italian water-based gold size (an adhesive for gilding) which has the immense advantage that it is ready to gild in 15-20 minutes but remains tacky for 36 hours, allowing the job to be completed the next day. Transfer leaf comes attached to little squares of transparent backing paper. The sheets are cut just a little larger than the area to be leafed, using scissors or a sharp knife, and then laid, slightly overlapping, metal leaf to size. After smoothing with the fingers the backing paper is peeled away, leaving the leaf stuck firmly to the sized area. Finally the whole gilded area is smoothed flat with a soft brush and dusted free of 'skewings'. Dutch Metal is brighter than gold leaf; too bright, Belinda decided, rubbing it over with fine wire wool to distress and break up the shine a little.

Lastly the piece was varnished. 'I give a piece as many coats as I think it is likely to need. On this I thought two coats would be enough, and I chose Craig and Rose Extra Pale Dead Flat because I didn't want to spoil my soft watercolour effect by shining it up. I thin the first varnish coat with white spirit and brush it on with the grain. On a piece that is going to get a lot of wear I might apply two coats of gloss polyurethane varnish first, then, after keying with fine sandpaper, a coat of matt to finish. This gives a subtle depth to colours, without shine.'

After leaving the varnish to harden up for two weeks or longer, Belinda likes to finish a painted piece with a slightly tinted wax to give it patina and a look of age.

Lastly the handles and escutcheons were replaced. 'I was trying to remember why I used gold rather than silver leaf – I love silver with blue – and then I remembered – it was because the piece had brass handles, and the gilding had to match.'

COLOURED GLAZES

CAVE ART
COMES TO TOWN

To Lesley Ruda, painting furniture is the jam; the bread and butter she earns painting walls, ceilings and staircases, murals and marbling and much besides. South African born, she has travelled widely in Europe and elsewhere looking, learning and painting, and she is currently in the USA sharing her skills with those of a cabinet-maker in Los Angeles. Her painted pieces are one-offs, junk finds such as the old filing cabinet shown here, which she works on obsessively, layering colours, glazes and decorative techniques until they surely would not recognize themselves, and they often fetch up with a highish price tag in a posh shop or gallery. But though she paints furniture to sell on, not having a fixed abode at present, it is not for the money she does it so much as for the creative journey she embarks on with each piece, which takes her round museums and libraries, researching designs and details to be worked into what art historians would call her 'iconography' or symbolic narrative.

The original inspiration for the extraordinary transformation wrought on an ordinary old wooden filing cabinet were some cave paintings she saw in Zimbabwe, and stored in her memory for future use. Cave paintings on a filing cabinet? 'I liked the idea of transferring these ancient images from inside a damp dark cave on to the outside of something functional and usable today,' she explains.

The story, or narrative, welding the decorative elements together is immensely important to her; what is unusual, perhaps, is the degree to which her craft always comes in to support her art.

For instance, she says crisply of the filing cabinet, 'It is always worth looking for something quality-made to work on. Just think what it would cost you today to get something made with all those drawers in wood.'

And she respects the ritual of proper preparation of a piece for painting. The handles of the drawers were removed, and the whole piece stripped of its

Left: An astonishing pillar in blue and gold is what a painterly imagination has created from the sort of filing cabinet you wouldn't look at twice if you passed it on the pavement outside an office equipment shop. Though Lesley Ruda's ideas are often unorthodox, and her techniques innovative, the workmanship is always impeccable.

dark varnish with methylated spirit and wire wool; a spot of paint stripper helped with the refractory bits.

The niche in the drawer stack came about because one of her ideas was to insert a clock face and turn the piece into a surreal grandfather-filing cabinet. This did not work out, so she had another idea – to extract two drawers, reinsert the one above the niche upside down, and instal concealed lighting there to make a little inside cave where something could stand. Eccentric perhaps, but a pointer to the creative approach to recycling junk.

MATERIALS

1 litre acrylic primer; 1 litre off-white eggshell oil-based paint; transparent oil glaze; white spirit; artists' oil tube colours in raw umber, raw sienna, viridian, Prussian blue, burnt sienna; gold powders in yellow and reddish tones; standard shellac for sealing; Spectraflow medium; acrylic tube colours in alizarin crimson, vermilion, burnt sienna; sheet of bubble wrap; Craig and Rose Extra Pale Dead Flat Varnish; assorted artists' brushes, including a stencil brush; standard decorating brush; varnish brush; fine and medium grade sandpaper.

METHOD

First the piece was given two coats of acrylic primer on the exterior and inside the niche. This was rubbed down with sandpaper to make a smooth base for two or three coats of off-white eggshell, making a non-absorbent base for decoration with oil glazes.

Lesley emphasizes that she did not start with the final effect in mind; ideas came as she went along. The first, simpler, intention was to finish the cabinet in stony, raw umber colour, to suggest the Zimbabwe cave walls. She used raw umber and raw sienna glazes sponged on with a natural sponge, randomly, then softened off with a brush, also randomly. However, this

Above: The cave painting inspiration for Lesley's piece shows up dramatically in this eland head with its glowing almond eye based on prehistoric cave art (some believe it was painted by Bushmen) near Zimbabwe.

looked too restrained. Lesley decided she needed to bring in the effect of underwater colour, as in the caves. Once the stone effect was dry she sponged over it with a succession of blue oil glazes, working from light to intense, sponging the colours on, and then wiping off here and there to let the stone colours show through.

She used cartridge paper, wiped over with fast-drying PVA (from builders' merchants) to waterproof it, to cut her own stencils, based on the cave drawings. These she stencilled on with a stencil brush and a mixture of blue and burnt sienna glaze colour for a soft, transparent effect, arranging them randomly as in the caves.

The cabinet was already well metamorphosed, but at this stage Lesley decided that a metallic element was needed – molten gold. 'I wanted the idea of volcanic fire spurting through the rock.'

Ever practical, she first coated the entire work to date with standard shellac to protect it from subsequent experimentation – she was not yet certain what form this would take. She also rubbed the shellac coat when dry with fine wire wool to smooth it and knock back the shine.

She wanted the gold to streak over the surfaces randomly, not as if sponged or rubbed or brushed on. After some experiment she discovered Spectraflow, a medium not unlike scumble glaze or gold size, which gave the effect she wanted.

Laying the cabinet flat so as to work on a horizontal surface, she made 'little pools' of Spectraflow on the surface here and there. Using two colours of gold powder, lemon and red gold, she combined various ways of adding it to the Spectraflow (acting here as a size, or fixative).

'Sometimes I dropped it on the pools, sometimes I put it in a spoon and blew it across the pools, so it got a natural drifting look, with no edges. I found the Spectraflow set off quite quickly, so as each face of the cabinet dried I turned it over and worked on another. The top I simply sponged with gold powder in shellac. And I used a brush in the gold/shellac solution to work over the handles.'

The inside of the niche and the drawer mouldings she coloured with acrylic tube colours, because by now she was in a hurry to see the piece complete, and acrylic dries fast. She used reds – crimson and vermilion alternately – first, then two coats of burnt sienna for an earthy warmth.

She felt the niche also needed the life of a little gold, but 'wild gold' as on the outside of the cabinet. Mixing up a brown red glaze (burnt sienna/alizarin/scumble glaze), she brushed this on and, while just wet, textured it with bubble wrap, pushing this into the glaze to make a pattern which was not uniform. Into these 'bubbles' she jabbed a little gold on a brush, and softened it off slightly. 'I just wanted it patchy.'

She is proud of the bubble wrap idea, her own invention. Improvisation often opens up new possibilities in decorative painting, much as it does in cooking. Thus the updated contribution to traditional ragrolling with cotton rag or chamois leather is 'bagging' with a scrumpled plastic bag. The message is: paint techniques should not become ossified. To protect her highly wrought and mysterious decorative treatment, she gave the whole cabinet, outside and inside, two coats of Craig and Rose Extra Pale Dead Flat Varnish, which is by far the most popular finishing medium in the contemporary decorative painter's arsenal.

Lastly, she rubbed over the surfaces with a pale beeswax polish, and buffed this up to a very discreet lustre.

'I usually finish a piece with wax,' she says. 'I like the patination this gives, and the little extra colour.'

GOLDWORK

PATRICIA RICHARDS' ELDORADO

Made redundant after 20 years of teaching art, Patricia Richards had the gumption to recognize that as one door closes, another may beckon invitingly. She had always wanted more time to develop her own decorative ideas and saw this as a chance to do something just for herself.

Happening on ideal premises – a disused schoolbuilding in north Wales which provides her with studio, stockroom and a 'rather off the beaten track showroom' for her work – Patricia planted climbers against every brick wall in sight and settled down to devote herself to 'goldwork'. This is her own term for her striking gold-on-black decorative painting on furniture, much influenced by traditional lacquer as well as 18th-century japanning, but carried out entirely with modern commercial products. Trial and error over the past six years has resulted in a working method and blend of products which give the effect she wants without requiring the endless layers, burnishing and varnishing of the traditional finishes. While the black base may not have the sumptuous texture of the old lacquers, it is remarkable what a subtle range of effects and tints she obtains from corner-cutting gold paints and varnishes which in most hands look gaudy or even garish. The materials may be time-savers but this is scrupulously detailed painting, each leaf and petal limned and shaded. Her devotion to her subject undoubtedly shows, but it also means that 'goldwork' does not exactly zip along – subjects as lavish as the bouquets shown here, with their hovering butterfly halo, easily swallow up 40 discontinuous hours of work and a chest of drawers may take between 24 and 30 hours. Work such as this cannot be for a mass market, so Patricia works mostly to commission.

Though she has recently been trying out her goldwork on coloured glazed backgrounds, Patricia works largely in gold on black. 'I like it because it is very dramatic,' she says. 'That's a personal thing.' She spends a lot of time researching old and traditional subjects and pieces to use for inspiration. She hunts for these in books and saleroom catalogues, as well as museum and

Left: What Patricia Richards calls 'my goldwork' gives considerable splendour to a remarkable four poster bed with a swan-neck finial on the headboard. None of the 'gold' is actually gold leaf; but with practice Patricia has learnt how to give metallic waxes and paints the soft lustre of the real thing.

stately home leaflets and postcards, and keeps a sketchbook of pencilled details spotted on her travels.

While the style is firmly traditional, the furniture Patricia paints, like the materials she uses, is new – mostly pine reproduction pieces from a range she has found well made and reliable, produced nearby in Newark. Occasionally the urge to do a spectacular showpiece such as the decorated four-poster bed sends her to consult a craftsman in North Devon who has been making beds for 30 years and is a mine of information and suggestions. The four-poster, with its turned posts and finials and swan-neck headboard, is a historical composite, fruit of this happy collaboration.

'I told him I didn't want to rely on hangings, it was to be a *painted* four-poster – an American idea,' says Patricia. 'He advised on the shape of the posts and finials, which are made of Douglas fir. The head and foot are of one inch ply, with a veneered edge for smoothness. He even makes little turned plugs to cover the bolts when the bed is assembled!'

Painstaking decoration like hers needs a reliable foundation. She sometimes paints furniture made of MDF (medium density fibreboard), which she likes for its stability – 'it isn't subject to expansion and contraction, like wood,' but finds too heavy to use for large items.

MATERIALS

Sand-and-seal shellac; medium and fine grade sandpaper; fine grade wire wool; patent knotting; 1 litre dark grey undercoat; 1 litre black eggshell paint; 1 litre clear matt polyurethane varnish; varnish brush.

Goldwork Yellow ochre artists' oil tube colour; white spirit; Connoisseur Treasure Gold metallic waxes in various shades, including pink, blue, green, Florentine gold and bronze; Connoisseur Treasure Sealer; Connoisseur Brush Bath; Liberon Gilt Varnish in Chantilly and Trianon; mixed hair signwriters' brushes for fine work, sizes 0 and 00; for larger areas, Winsor and Newton Sceptre 101 range, sizes 1-8.

METHOD

On new pine any knots are sealed with patent knotting to prevent resin 'weeping' through the paint finish. Disliking primer, Patricia seals surfaces with a special sand-and-seal shellac, one coat for pine, two for absorbent MDF. After sanding down with medium grade sandpaper to get a silky surface, she paints the piece with two coats of undercoat, followed by two coats of black eggshell paint, rubbing down gently but thoroughly between coats when hard dry. She goes over this black base next with clear matt polyurethane varnish – a very important step to protect the finish if she needs to make any alterations to the gold decoration.

Patricia sketches her design on to the dry varnish using yellow ochre oil colour thinned with white spirit and leaves this to dry overnight. The next morning, in a state of some anticipation, she begins going over the sketched shapes and details with Treasure Gold. She applies it with a brush, or her fingertips for a different effect, changing shades – bronze, Florentine, etc. – for variety. These Treasure Gold colours need frequent shaking to redistribute the metallic powder content, otherwise the paint loses its lustre and body. She does not lay the colours on too thickly, however. They dry almost instantly, but should be sealed with Treasure Sealer before applying any other process, be it Liberon Gilt Varnish or polyurethane, because the solvents in these would attack the waxy content of the Treasure Gold paints. The sealer, too, is left to dry hard.

Left: Elaborate ornament like the chinoiserie inspired bouquets on this bed can look static, which is one reason why Patricia likes to dot in tiny expressive bird shapes, or butterflies and other insects. She collects motifs in a sketchbook which she consults before starting on a new project.

Patricia often finds the colours look too brash and gaudy when she comes back to the piece so she goes over the goldwork with Liberon Gilt Varnish in various shades – Trianon and Chantilly are current favourites – to soften it. With a fine brush she paints over the sealed Treasure Gold to give it something of the 'texture of fabric, like old brocade almost'. For an even softer effect she thins the Gilt Varnish with white spirit. When she wants to emphasize details, outlines, feathers etc. she dips her fine brush into the thick waxy substance at the bottom of the Gilt Varnish jar and uses this to produce a bright gold line with a slightly raised texture, giving a very rich effect. She may complete a decoration in one burst of effort or go back to it repeatedly, adding and subtracting, putting in touches of metallic colour, shading with darker metal tones, often smoothed on with a fingertip for softness. Every time the Treasure Gold is used it is sealed again with the Treasure Sealer, and the brushes are washed out in the Brush Bath.

Treasure Sealer dries with a high gloss. When Patricia wants the piece to have a smooth matt finish, as in the case of the four-poster, she gives it four coats of clear matt polyurethane varnish; she thins the first two coats and rubs the surface of the third coat silky smooth with very fine wire wool, taking care to brush off any clinging shreds of steel wool before applying the final coat of varnish.

ACRYLIC PAINTS
HOMMAGE A HENRI

Matthew Lauder has been a devotee of Henri Matisse, that supreme colourist, since his student days doing fine art at Camberwell. In 1990 he visited Paris with his mother, also an artist, to have another look at the great man's work, and the copy of *Girl in Embroidered Blouse* on the wall is a souvenir of the trip which he painted for her shortly afterwards. He has had an exhibition of his own paintings and Matisse, he admits, was 'a big influence. I'm a linear painter too.'

Like a good percentage of art school graduates, Matthew does 'finishes' to pay the mortgage. Four years of painting scenery at the National Theatre with 6 inch/16 cm brushes and compressor spray guns beefed up his muscles and taught him 'a feeling for scale, and a lot of techniques'. His decorative work is loose and gutsy rather than careful and refined, and the stage painting experience shows in his preference for fast-drying acrylic and emulsion paints used to bold effect.

When painting a wooden bench came up as his Masterclass project, it was inevitable that he should think once more of Matisse. 'Not just because I love him but because he's really good for someone copying because of his flat, linear quality. Also I wanted to do something bright, and his colours are wonderful.'

The result is a spirited rendering of *Odalisque aux Camellias* so arranged that the houri lounges invitingly along the bench back, with her bowl of oranges, as in the painting, beside her but on a different plane, on the seat. He has also extended the odalisque's striped rug right to the edge of the bench. 'I liked the way the bench curves round at the edge, like a mattress. So when you sit on the bench it's a bit as if you were sitting on the edge of her bed. I thought that was nicely jokey.'

To make sure of getting the proportions of the copy right he used a technique that ensures success; he took a slide of the original painting and

Left: A perfectly ordinary hall bench goes over the top with gusto when it receives a voluptuous odalisque sprawled across the back and a still life of oranges on the seat. Imitation is the sincerest form of flattery; Matthew Usmar Lauder is passionately attached to Matisse. He also thinks he is one of the easier painters to copy successfully.

151

projected the image on to the bench, moving it around until 'she seemed to fit the space'. Mural painters sometimes use projectors to flash architectural subjects on to walls, where they can be traced 'from the life', as it were. This method is a bit of a cheat but it guarantees accuracy and saves time; it is especially helpful when painting *trompe l'oeil* subjects, where realism counts for everything.

MATERIALS

Medium grade sandpaper; Liquitex acrylic gesso; wide range of acrylic artists' oil tube colours; selection of artists' brushes in the larger sizes; soft pencil; slide and slide projector; 1 litre terracotta matt emulsion; standard paint brush; Craig and Rose Extra Pale Dead Flat Varnish; varnish brush.

METHOD

The small wooden bench, of a type designed at the beginning of the century to stand in hallways with storage space under the lift-up seat, was already painted with a creamy white paint which only needed sanding with medium grade sandpaper to provide a good base for the acrylic gesso which Matthew used as primer under acrylic colours.

Matthew only intended the 'Matisse' to cover the back and seat, so he skipped gessoing the legs and base. He left the choice of colour for them until the end as well; colour decisions of this sort are best left till last, when what has already been done more or less dictates the choice of a suitable shade.

He gave the back and seat of the bench two coats of fast-drying acrylic gesso to provide a good surface for paint. This was rubbed down, not too finely, to give a texture approximating canvas. Matthew painted directly on to the gesso base but he thinks another time he would have started by painting it a mid tone, like a dark flesh tone. 'People who wanted to try

something like this might find it easier putting lights and darks on to a mid tone than on to all that glaring white, which looks so much at first.'

Then, setting up the slide projector, he flashed the odalisque on to the bench, moving it about until the position and scale felt right. Then, with a pencil, he drew round the picture shapes as projected on to the bench.

'I just used this for the main outlines, so that everything was located correctly. After that it was freehand all the way,' he says.

Working with a printed reproduction beside him on the bench to check colours and detail, he began blocking in colour quite loosely. He chose acrylic colours because he is used to working with them, and their speed of drying compresses a project like this into a fraction of the time Matisse's oil media would have needed. 'I know oils are much richer, but I think I can match their effect quite closely with acrylics if I varnish over the work to give more depth to the colours.'

He began with the draped odalisque herself, her navel neatly located between the ridges of a narrow moulding used to frame inset panels on the bench back. Matthew simply painted these mouldings out, which gives the painted lady floating across them a touch of the surreal.

'I worked hard to get her face right,' he says. 'I used a small brush for her features because by Matisse's standards they are quite finely detailed.'

For the flesh tones he experimented with the warm siennas, using them, as Matisse had done, to model a series of luxuriant curves, languidly erotic. Like Goya's *Naked Maja*, this lady is all invitation. The white drapery used the gesso base, as did the magnolias, though these needed a little warming with creamy ochre.

Left: It is always surprising to find what the eye will calmly accept as long as it is boldly presented. The best way to treat inconveniences like mouldings is to ignore them, it seems.

the change of plane, but it must be said that it enhances the slightly surreal quality of an odalisque with a fold down the middle. Besides, the superb turquoise bowl of ruddy oranges, on which Matthew lavished his best brushwork, does make a nice thing to look at when you are sitting on the bench – if you can tear your eyes away from that oddly compelling stare from over your right shoulder, that is.

Extending the green and yellow stripes of the original to cover the seat were really the only additions Matthew made to Matisse's subject matter. He did these freehand, scorning masking tape, but with some care so that they fan out smoothly and dramatically over the seat, leading the eye into the picture.

For the base he experimented with various shades of red to terracotta, finally mixing up a vivid scarlet that picks up the scarlet bands behind the lady, the checks beneath her, and the warm flesh tones. The base was painted in matt emulsion – two coats for opacity. Then the whole piece was given two coats of Craig and Rose varnish to give more depth to the acrylic colours, which have a 'flat' effect, as well as to protect a striking metamorphosis of wooden hall bench. The *faux* flagstones in the foreground were dashed in at the last minute in true stage-painter style to offset all this vivid colour.

The background colour is a splendid, complex purple-brown-red. Matthew mixed this and brushed it on, then brushed over it with a slightly darker, colder version of the same shade to give a painterly texture. Adding the bold, characteristic touches of the master, the firm curving outlines of magnolias and leaves, the sky blue brushstrokes to the right of her raised knee, and the pink-on-red (a favourite Matisse combination) checks beneath her was sheer delight.

The stripes on the back and seat were now blocked in, and a fold of greenish gold drapery and a bowl of glowing oranges rounded off the picture. Matisse might not have approved of

TROMPE L'OEIL
THE WITTY BRUSH

Tall, flaxen and unmistakably Anglo-Saxon, Nemone Burgess came to decorative painting with the briefest formal training.

'One was allowed a term at the Byam Shaw by one's rather Victorian parents,' she says. To this modicum of instruction she later added a marbling and graining course, 'years before everyone did it', and a valuable stint working alongside a 'painter of the old school who taught me the principles of decorating'.

Talent, industry and the instinctive taste and flair needed to excel in a competitive trade have put her among the top practitioners in this country today. Her graining skills are celebrated – she is currently working on ideas for a Biedermeyer-style combination of dark and pale grained panels for one of the royal libraries. Painted loo seats are another speciality, providing her with four separate opportunities for visual jokes and surprises.

'There's the cover, front and back, and the seat. That's the ladies' share of the contraption. But of course gents lift the seat, so underneath is where one puts one's best jokes.'

Friends have suggested that instead of tearing up and down ladders growing callouses on her painting hand, Nemone should sit comfortably in her basement workshop turning out witty painted loo seats. The suggestion is dismissed with a snort.

'But what sort of loo seats, and for whom? There is almost no point in painting furniture if you don't know the person it is for and where it is going to go – at least that's my view,' she says firmly.

This applies particularly to another branch of the decorative painter's skills where the Burgess touch triumphs – an exercise in *trompe l'oeil* in the 18th-century manner, building up a coded portrait or character sketch of the client in question by assembling a collection of painted clues and private references which are decorative in themselves, but only yield their full

Left: The books are real, the handles are real and this is a real library table you are looking at, but everything else you see belongs to the world of painted illusion of trompe l'oeil. *Even, amazingly enough, the brass mesh on the door is painted.*

meaning to friends and relations. The *trompe l'oeil* composition on the library table shown here was commissioned by a friend and was paid for in champagne, 'for the good reason that I took so long over it that costing it seriously would have been impossible'. Her friend is a photographer, has been twice married, has several children, and is something of a bon vivant; all these events and characteristics are alluded to in the assemblage of pretty things reproduced with such skill and finesse by the witty Burgess brush.

'It is – I hope – the kind of piece that will get passed down through the family, and speculated about in the way things like this are, because they mean something to the family members,' she suggests, with characteristic diffidence.

The table itself is modern – a reproduction, mainly in MDF, of a family piece. The leather-bound books to left and right, below, are real, but the brass grille in the middle is entirely 'tromped', quite needlessly as Nemone admits, since a slice of the real thing was easily available and would have saved her hours of repetitive work. But *trompe* of this calibre is gloriously obsessive, and its own reward.

The skills required for this sort of high-fidelity representation in paint have to be worked for, but technology has an impact on the painter's approach and technique which is, of course, photography.

'Since it was for a photographer, it was easy. I made a mock-up of cardboard, painted green, for the top and arranged the things on it. He photographed them so I knew where the shadows and light fell.' Once armed with the photographs, and the objects themselves, Nemone began work on the table.

MATERIALS

Wood primer; oil-based undercoat; white shellac; transparent oil glaze; artists' oil tube colours in a wide range of colours; white spirit; Translac clear varnish; white polish; a sheaf of brushes, including some favourite Chinese ones.

METHOD

The table was delivered 'naked' – i.e. without primer or base coat – into Nemone's hands, though many decorative painters insist on pieces being delivered in a ready-to-go situation and this obviously saves clients money. She primed, sanded and undercoated the whole table using two different-coloured undercoats, cream for the base, dark green for the top. These surfaces were then sealed with a thinned coat of white shellac for smoothness. Over this went much-thinned transparent oil glazes tinted with the appropriate oil colours; 'baby oak leaf green' over the main body of the table, lightly dragged, and a darker green over the top to be 'tromped'.

The delicate 'laurel leaf' motif was painted freehand round the table top and the various crests and coronets added to the drawers in gold transfer leaf were overpainted in both raw and burnt umber. The brass grille was painted with gold powder in shellac, and antiqued in richer tones of burnt umber and sienna.

The *trompe l'oeil* work was tackled methodically, one object at a time. In effect each *trompe* is a careful portrait, in oils, of the object, which Nemone had beside her as she worked, together with the photograph showing the overall composition (vital for scale) and the critical direction, shape and intensity of the various shadows and highlights.

Trompe l'oeil is a refined form of faking, whose success depends on penetrating observation plus the experience to translate this into paint. As every professional *trompe* painter knows, the most convincingly three-dimensional objects (such as the coloured marble eggs here with their flawless gleam and modelling) are not necessarily the most difficult to render.

Above: The most technically difficult object to reproduce of the brilliantly painted group shown here was the theatre programme on the right.

'The hardest thing, unbelievably difficult in fact, was the oldish, brownish programme for *Oh What a Lovely War.*' This was a coded allusion to the client's first wife, who was an actress. Nemone spent hours working up the precise colour, texture and typography of the original souvenir programme. This difficulty was only matched by the problem of reproducing an entire copperplate wedding invitation to the client's second marriage to an aristocrat's daughter with a penchant for tatting and collecting marble eggs. Surprisingly, she used a brush – 'whisker fine' – for the copperplate, where lesser beings might have resorted to a Rotring drawing pen.

'It took forever,' she says feelingly, and, resisting the urge to snatch it up off the table for a closer look (the double take *trompe* painters live for) one can well believe this.

Contrast, not simply of colour or scale but also of style or value, is important to the charm of sophisticated *trompe*; the humble presence of the roll of film, the sauce whisk and the playing cards among various posh playthings adds lustre and credibility. Anything too sparkly and expensive is a vulgarity to avoid in the fastidious world of *trompe*.

I had two *trompe divertissements* painted in my own house by Paul and Janet Czainski many years ago for a television series. One, on the floor, brilliantly mimics a £10 note and is believed in my family to have finally broken the morale of a bunch of teenage burglars who sped through the place looking in every likely place cash might be secreted, such as teapots, boxes, loose floorboards, under mattresses. However, the caches were cashless, and the *trompe* tenner must have had a cynically joky impact far beyond its original intention. The second *trompe* was one that caught me out every time; it simply showed an ordinary steel screw 2 inches (5 cm) long, carelessly left on a windowsill – an annoying intrusion which I kept trying to tidy away, until finally, exasperated, I am ashamed to say I painted it over, the same colour as the sill.

Such is the insidious make-believe of the *trompe l'oeil* painter, barbed with a touch of malice, insight and wit.

Nemone Burgess always finds it difficult to remember the precise details of how she painted a *trompe* and with what colours. Each job is worked on and lived with obsessively, a constant preoccupation at the back or forefront of her mind. Once captured, for posterity one hopes, the crystallized images live on in their own world of make-believe.

Nemone finished by giving the whole table two or three coats of her favourite Translac varnish, clear, tough, and almost non-yellowing, to seal it and keep it safe for the amusement of future generations.

INDEX

Page numbers in italic *refer to the illustrations*

acetone, 132

acrylic paints, *150-3*, 151-3

acrylic primer, 25

Adam, Robert, 12, 20

'alligatoring', crackle glaze, 9, 59

aluminium primer, 25

Art Deco, 30, *34*, 65, 66, 96

arte povera, 8

Arts and Crafts Movement, 17

'bagging', 145

Bakst, Leon, 30

Ballantyne, Belinda, 24, *138-40*, 139-41

Ballets Russes, 30

Baroque style, 30, *30-1*

baskets: verdigris, 89, 90, *92-3*

woodwash, *112*, 113-15, *115-17*

beds, goldwork, *146*, 148, *149*

beeswax, 33, 37

Bell, Vanessa, 20, 131-2

benches, *150-3*, 151-3

Bennison, Geoffrey, 77-8

Bosschaert, 17

Boucher, François, 20

Boulle, 8

boxes: *faux* marquetry, 76, 80-1

penwork, 83-4

brushes, 28, *28-9*, 41-2

bureau, Scandinavian-style, *138-40*, 139-41

Burges, William, 13, 20, *21*, 96

Burgess, Nemone, *154-7*, 155-7

Burne-Jones, Edward, 13, 17

cabinets, sponging, *106-11*, 107-9

Campling, Robert, *130-3*, 131-3

casein-based paints, 33

cast iron, verdigris, *88*, 89-91, *90*

caustic soda, 24-5

cave paintings, 143, *144*

chairs, 26-7

marbling, *70*, 72-3, *74-5*

spattering, *118*, 120-1, *122*

verdigris, *88*, 89-91, *90*

Chambers, Sir William, 11

Charleston, Sussex, 131-2, 133

chests, *52-7*, 53-5

China, lacquerwork, 10

Chippendale, Thomas, 11

Cipriani brothers, 20

Claude Lorrain, 8, 84

cleaning brushes, 28

'clouds marbling', 72

coachpainting, 18

Colefax, Sybil, 21

Colefax and Fowler, 21

colours, *30-5*

aristocratic tradition, 12-13

Baroque/Georgian, *30-1*

combing, 55

crackle glazes, 60

folk/provincial tradition, 14-15

opacity, 33

Provençal, *32-3*

spattering, 120

sponging, 107-8

stains, 48

traditional, 30, *30-1*

transparent, 34, *34-5*

verdigris, 89

combing, *52-7*, 53-5

combs, *29*

commodes, 41-3, *44-5*

Copydex, *29*

coromandel, 10

Crace, Frederick, 20

crackle glaze, 9, *58-63*, 59-61, *134-6*, 135-7

craquelure, 59, 60, *134-6*, 135-7

'curtaining', 60

Czainski, Paul and Janet, 157

Darly, Matthew, 13

decoupage, 17

Delaney, Mrs, 17

desks, *46-51*, 47-50, *94*, 95-7, *98-9*

distemper, 33

distressing, 9

verdigris, *88-93*, 89-91

woodwash, 115, *117*

draggers, 54

dragging, *faux* marquetry, 79

'dry' paint finishes, *130-3*, 131-3

Dunand, Jean, 65

Empire style, 30

engravings, penwork, 83-4

erasers, *29*

faux lacquer, *64-9*, 65-7

faux marquetry, *76-81*, 77-9

feathers, *28*, 73

filing cabinet, *142-4*, 143-5

filling, 25

finishing agents, 36-7

floggers, 54

flowers, 16-17

foam pads, *29*, 96, 97, *98*

folk art, 14-15

Fowler, John, 21

France, 12

• François, André, 102

French polish, 24, 36
Fry, Roger, 20

garden furniture, verdigris, *88*, 89-91, *90*
Garrick, David, 11
Georgian colours, *30-1*
gesso, 114, *117*, 132, 137
gilding, 55, 137, 141
glazes: coloured, *142-4*, 143-5
    combing, 53, 55, 57
    crackle glaze, *58-63*, 59-61
    faux lacquer, 66
    faux marquetry, 79
    stippling, *40-5*, *41-3*
Gledhill, Charles, 135
goldwork, *146-9*, *147-9*
Gothic screen, *134-6*, *135-7*
grain filler, 25
graining, 9, 128-9
Grant, Duncan, 20, 131-3
Gray, Eileen, 11, 21, 65
Greece, 16
Hallingdal, *72*
Heal, Ambrose, 48
Henry III, King, 95-6
Hepplewhite, George, 13, 17
Hoffmann, Josef, 48
Howett, Jim, *134-5*, 135, 137

Indian ink, 85
ink, penwork, 8-9, 78-9, *82-7*, 83-5, *126-8*, *127-9*
Isopon, 25
Italy, 12, 16
ivory, carved, 83, 86

japanning, *10*, 11, 12, 18
Joel, Betty, 21

Kauffmann, Angelica, 20
Kennedy, Marianna, *134-6*, 135-7
knives, 29

lacquerwork, 8, 10-11, 12, 18, 19, 21
    faux lacquer, *64-9*, 65-7
Lanvin, Jeanne, 21
latticed effects, 41, *41*
Lauder, Matthew, *150-3*, 151-3
library table, *trompe l'oeil*, *154-7*, 156-7
liming, *46-51*, 47-50
lining, 43
Lutyens, Edwin, 13

Mackintosh, Charles Rennie, 17, 20
malachite, 8
marbling, 8, *70-5*, 71-3
marquetry, *76-81*, 77-9
marriage chests, 14
Martin brothers, 11
masking fluid, 78
masking tape, *28*
Matisse, Henri, 151-3
Maugham, Syrie, 21
Messel, Oliver, 48
methylated spirits, 24
mirror frame, penwork, *82*, 83, 84, *86-7*
Moguls, 16
Morris, William, 13, 17, 20, 96

Nash, John, 20
Netherlands, 17
Norway, 139-40

office furniture, *46-51*, 47-50
Omega Group, 20-1, 30, 131-3
opaque colours, 33
paint stripper, 24
papie mâché, 17, 18
Parker, George, *10*, 11, 17
patination, verdigris, *88-93*, 89-91
pencils, *29*
pens, *29*, 78-9, 84, 85, 103
penwork, 8-9, 78-9, *82-7*, 83-5, *126-8*, *127-9*
Persia, 16
Phyfe, Duncan, 11
pietra dura, 9, *9*
Pillement, Jean, 13
Plaka casein-based paints, 33, 137
plastic wood, 25
Pompadour, Madame de, 11
Pontypool Ware, 17, 18
postcards, *trompe l'oeil*, *100*, 102-3, *103*, *105*
Poussin, Nicolas, 8, 84
'powdered' ornament, 95
priming, 25
proprietary strippers, 24
Provençal colours, *32-3*
pumices, 67

Rateau, 21
red oxide, 25
Regency colours, 30

Renaissance, 12, 16, 17
Richards, Patricia, *146-9*, 147-9
Romans, 16
Rotring pens, 29, 78-9, 84, 85, 103
rottenstone, 67
Ruda, Lesley, *142-4*, 143-5
Ruhlmann, 21
rulers, *29*
rust, 91, *93*

sand-and-seal shellac, 25
sanding, 24
sandpaper, 28, *28*
scalpels, *29*
Scandinavian style, 12-13, *138-40*, 139-41
scissors, *28*
screens, *134-6*, 135-7
'scrimshaw', 83
scumble glazes, 53
shadows, *trompe l'oeil*, 103, 105
shellac, 11, 18, 25, 36, 55, 85, 109
Sheraton, Thomas, 13, 17
size, 137
smoothing, 25
solvents, 24
Sotsass, Emilio, 21
spattering, *118-23*, 119-21
Spectraflow, 145
sponges, *29*
sponging, *106-11*, 107-9
staining, *46-51*, 47-50, 78, *81*
Stalker, John, *10*, 11, 17
stencilling, *77-8*, *81*, *94-9*, 95-7